# Victory Over Trial and Trouble

# E. Allen Griffith, D.D.

*Faithful Life Publishers*
*Lebanon, Pennsylvania*

Copyright 2004 by E. Allen Griffith, D.D.

ISBN 0-9749836-0-8

Published by Faithful Life Publishers
Lebanon, PA
faithfullifepublishers@hotmail.com

Cover photo: www.istockphoto.com
Cover design: Kara D. Sanger

Scripture quotations, unless otherwise noted, are from the Authorized King James Version of the Holy Bible.

Printed in the United States of America
13  12  11  10  09  08  07  06     2  3  4  5  6

*This book is dedicated to my wife, Tricia,
who walked by my side the night I went forward
to trust Jesus Christ as my Savior
and has continued steadfastly by my side
in facing each and every trial
the Lord has allowed along life's pathway.
I am grateful to God for her.*

# TABLE OF CONTENTS

# PREFACE

*Victory Over Trial and Trouble* (for those who really want victory) is primarily a Bible study of the significant texts of Scripture related to trials and heartache among people. It is intended for those who really want victory in their own lives. Some feel sorry for themselves because of all that has happened to them. They want an easy fix and just want to feel good again. If that is where you are, this book is not intended for you. Indeed, as you read this text it may make you angry at times, but I hope you will continue anyway. On the other hand, if you are tired of living in defeat and long to experience real joy and peace in your life, this book is for you. If in your heart you know you have been defeated, discouraged, and perhaps bitter at God or people but refuse to stay there any longer, this book is for you. This book will direct you to the Word of God and guide you to true spiritual victory—if you really want it.

It is hoped, as well, that this text will do more than help solve problems after the fact. May it provide spiritual strength and understanding of God and His truth so defeat will be prevented, in spite of the hard times that may come your way. This book will open up the opportunity for you to gain spiritual wisdom, so you can respond properly in the face of trial. The writers of Scripture were not offering untested theories. They were giving us Holy Spirit revelation to instruct us how to live.

This text will be suitable for personal study and discipleship as well as profitable as a text for a Bible study or Sunday School class. The Bible is filled with wonderful truth for the child of God as he faces the challenges of life in this sinful world. May this book serve to open hearts and minds to some of that precious truth.

# INTRODUCTION

Over my years of ministry I have seen an incredible amount of suffering in the lives of people. It has come in every form imaginable. As the suffering came, I watched people respond to their tragic experiences in a variety of ways. Some crumbled under the pressures of life—while others found strength in the Lord. Some pressed on, though carrying a heavy load of bitterness—while others moved forward discovering sweet and enduring victory through God's grace. Some questioned the love and justice of God—while others were comforted in His everlasting arms.

In all I have seen and experienced, TWO TRUTHS have settled deeply within my heart:

- The greatest test in a trying time is not what we go through, but how we respond to it.

- Our response to trial makes the difference in what that trial will ultimately produce in our lives.

You may be reading this book because you are going through a terrible time of hurt and heartache. If so, I hope you will take comfort in this truth. You are not alone. As the Apostle Peter wrote in I Peter 5:9, "…knowing that the same afflictions are accomplished in your brethren that are in the world." Others have gone through what you are facing and have found victory in the power, grace, and love of God. That same victory is available to you.

It is important to understand that victory is not to be equated with a change in circumstances. For some the circumstances do not change. The disease afflicting the body is not always healed. The loved one who has passed away is not coming back. The unkind person may or may not change. However, in the midst of the most difficult trials stands the promise of God in Hebrews 13:5, "I will never leave thee, nor forsake thee." Experiencing the fullness of that promise is where we find our victory. If you are wearied and broken, perhaps in the midst of discouragement, but you really want help, it is available to you. David wrote in Psalm 40:1-2, "I waited patiently for the Lord; and he inclined unto me, and heard my cry. He brought me up also out of an horrible pit, out of the miry clay, and set my feet upon a rock, and established my goings." This same victory can be yours through believing and obeying the Word of God.

While much Scripture is quoted in this book, you will want to get your Bible, open it to the various passages, and reflect on the teachings you will receive.

# CHAPTER ONE

# THE SUFFERING PEOPLE ENDURE

Suffering comes in many forms. It includes physical pain, emotional hurt, mental stress, and spiritual attack. I am sure I am not telling you anything you do not already know. Not only does trouble come in a variety of forms, but it also comes from a variety of sources. It may be rooted in Satanic attack. It might originate with unkind or evil people. It might result from physical disease and injury or perhaps from a variety of other circumstances, some of which we may even bring upon ourselves.

All of these trials are found recorded in the Bible in the lives of real people just like you and me. Perhaps you will find your situation recorded in the life of a person who lived in Bible times. As you read this section, you will see illustrations of what others have endured. You may find something similar to what you have faced or you may find the exact same experience. May your first touch of comfort come from seeing what Peter says: "The same afflictions (that you are enduring) are accomplished in your brethren that are in the world." **Others have been where you are!**

### 1. People have lost loved ones in death.

- David (II Samuel 18:33), Mary—the mother of Jesus (John 19:25–30), and Naomi (Ruth 1:3–5) all lost children in death. Many have said to lose a child is the toughest loss. The parent is "supposed" to die before the child.

- Lot lost his wife as she turned to view the judgment on Sodom. (Genesis 19:23–26)

- Naomi, Ruth, and Orpah lost their husbands. No cause of their deaths is recorded. (Ruth 1:3–5)

· Mary and Martha lost their brother. (John 11:1–21)

· David lost his dearest friend, Jonathan. (II Samuel 1:25–27)

We know that it is "appointed unto men once to die." Should our Savior tarry each of us will die leaving loved ones behind or we will stand by as our loved ones precede us to the grave. I have always marveled that Jesus wept at the grave of Lazarus, even though He knew He would shortly call him back to life. Death is "the wage of sin," and, though we may be sure of heaven as born-again Christians, death to someone close to us can strike us with a terrible sting and agonizing emptiness.

### 2. People have been betrayed by loved ones and friends.

· Hosea was betrayed in unfaithfulness by his wife. (Hosea 2:1–5)

· Esau was betrayed in deceit by his brother, Jacob. (Genesis 27:1–41)

· Joseph was betrayed by his brothers, who sold him into slavery. (Genesis 37:28–36)

· Paul was betrayed by his friends. He said that "all had forsaken him." (II Timothy 4:16–17)

· The Lord Jesus was betrayed by Judas. (Mark 14:10–11)

Betrayal can be especially tough to bear because it implies deception by the very one in whom we have placed trust and confidence. The more we open our hearts to someone, the harder it is when they turn against us or seek to do us harm.

### 3. People have grown up in broken homes.

· When Ishmael was only 15 or 16 years of age, he and his mother, Hagar, were forced out of their home. Ishmael grew up without the security and care of two loving parents. His father was not there. (Genesis 21:8–21)

To grow up in a broken home seems unfair. Others have two parents to provide love and security, as well as spiritual and financial well-being. The child of the broken home often feels cheated in life. Indeed, he has been, but he must find victory over it.

### 4. People have endured terrible illness.

· The woman with the issue of blood suffered for 12 years. (Matthew 9:20–22)

· The woman with the spirit of infirmity was bent over, unable to stand up straight for 18 years. (Luke 13:10–13)

· The man with an infirmity had suffered 38 years. He endured the frustration of seeing others healed, while he was overlooked. (John 5:1–9)

Sickness touches us all at one time or another, but for some it is debilitating and (as illustrated above) can be long lasting. Sickness is not only a problem in itself, but it often hinders us from handling all the other pressures we are called upon to bear. How hard it can be to deal with financial problems, difficult people, or just getting through life when we are not physically well.

### 5. People have had great problems with childbirth.

· Sarah was unable to have children until the supernatural intervention of God allowed her to have Isaac when she was ninety years old. (Genesis 21:1–2)

· Bathsheba's baby died seven days after his birth. (II Samuel 12:18)

Little else can compare with the joy of bringing a healthy child into this world. How tragic when that anticipation and accompanying excitement is destroyed through the inability to bear children or the devastating loss of a child during pregnancy or shortly after birth. Others have given birth but have had to face physical or mental defects in their precious child. How do we pick up the pieces and go on?

### 6. People have suffered in poverty.

· The widow of Zarephath was so poor she was ready to prepare a small cake for herself and her son, expecting then to die of starvation. (I Kings 17:10–12)

· Lazarus was a child of God, but in poverty and sickness he had nothing to eat but the leftover garbage from the rich man's table.

In that terrible condition he lived his last days and died. (Luke 16:19–22)

One of the most common, though flawed, ideas among men is that if you do right you should be blessed financially by God. Not having *enough* money is a source of great discouragement for many people. Today, most people deal with the problem through the use of credit; but eventually debt catches up with the card user and then comes despair. It is not easy when we see others prospering.

### 7. *People have been sexually violated.*

· Tamar was raped by her half brother, Amnon. (II Samuel 13:1–14)

· Bathsheba was called to David's house where David committed adultery with her—while her husband was in the military fighting a war. (II Samuel 11:1–4)

Sensuality and immorality are dominating our culture. The result is a dramatic growth in sexually related sins and crimes, which in turn produce numerous victims. The commonness of the problem, however, does not relieve the devastating mental, emotional, and physical toll on those who are so abused. Sometimes offenders are family members or friends, which only worsens the situation and complicates resolution. Fear and shame often compel victims to keep their hurts to themselves. They suffer within and find no source of comfort or help. Is there victory available?

### 8. *People have been falsely accused.*

· Saul turned against David with many false accusations and then tried to kill him. (I Samuel 18:8–30)

· Ahab, the king, accused Elijah of being the one who troubled Israel—while the actual troublemaker was Ahab himself. (I Kings 18:17–18)

Bad news travels so much faster than good news. Even if innocence can be proven, how does one ever trace down the trail of stories to finally prove the real truth to all who have heard the lie? That the Devil is *the accuser of the brethren* testifies to the wicked origin of false accusations. A reputation before men may be harmed, but one must rest in God who knows the whole truth.

### 9. People have been defeated when trying to do right.

· Elijah thought he stood alone for God and battled against the wickedness of Ahab and Jezebel, but unfulfilled expectations and physical weariness thrust him into depression and discouragement. (I Kings 19:1–10)

· Paul sought only to serve the Lord but was driven out of many communities, stoned and left for dead, imprisoned, and finally died a martyr's death. (II Corinthians 11:24–27)

Human logic would dictate that seeking to do the right thing should be accompanied by success. When so many evildoers prosper, the frustration of failure (when trying to do right) can make us want to stop trying. The Bible warns us to *faint not* because God knows our tendency is to quit when things go wrong.

### 10. People have been persecuted for the Lord and His truth.

Hebrews 11:36–39 describes many who "had trial of cruel mockings and scourgings, yea, moreover of bonds and imprisonments: they were stoned, they were sawn asunder, were tempted, were slain with the sword: they wandered about in sheepskins and goatskins; being destitute, afflicted, tormented;(Of whom the world was not worthy): they wandered in deserts, and in mountains, and in dens and caves of the earth. And these all, having obtained a good report through faith, received not the promise."

Though Peter tells his readers in I Peter 4:12 to "think it not strange concerning the fiery trial which is to try you, as though some strange thing happened unto you," we are seldom prepared to suffer for the cause of Christ. A young lady we know was gloriously saved out of a life of sin and drug abuse. Her lost, though religious, father responded to her faith in Christ by announcing he would rather she had stayed on drugs. What a devastating remark to a new believer—but persecution should be expected. Paul told Timothy in II Timothy 3:12, "Yea, and all that will live godly in Christ Jesus shall suffer persecution." For some reason, suffering for Christ takes us by surprise, even though the Lord told us it would happen.

### 11. People have experienced the seeming collapse of everything.

· Job lost his children in death, lost virtually all his wealth, lost his health, had his friends turn against him, and finally his wife browbeat him in cynicism. (Job 1:13–2:9)

Only Job's spiritual perspective delivered him from total defeat when he lost everything. He rightly confessed in Job 1:21, "Naked came I out of my mother's womb, and naked shall I return thither: the Lord gave, and the Lord hath taken away; blessed be the name of the Lord." When everything seems to go wrong, it is easy for us to lose our perspective and fall into total gloom. Job did not, and we marvel at God's grace in his life.

### 12. One has suffered in total innocence.

· Only the Lord Jesus fits into the category of total innocence. (Isaiah 53:1–12)

At the same time, the cry of the world for all of time has been "Why do the innocent suffer?" Of course, we know from the Scriptures that none are innocent—indeed, "All have sinned and come short of the glory of God." We still struggle, however, when we look at some people who seem to do much wrong and suffer little, while others seem to do little wrong and suffer much. Only the Judgment Seat of Christ will reveal the whole story. Then we will understand. For now we are called upon "to walk by faith and not by sight."

If you are reading this book to seek help, you may very well be able to identify with one or more of the people listed above. Not everyone mentioned received victory (as you would see if you read their whole story), but they could have. Praise the Lord, **there is hope and there is help for those who really want it.** To find renewed hope and to get real help, you must follow the Scriptures carefully—for they are the very Word of God. There are no hidden secrets to be discovered. The message is somewhat simple—trust and obey. Believe what they say, do what they tell you to do, and you can find greater victory than you might have ever imagined possible.

In the following pages we will examine many aspects of those heartbreaking trials we go through and we will see what is involved in trusting and obeying. We will not be able to address every kind of trial in detail but the principles we explore are applicable to every situation. Through prayerful surrender to God's Word, you can get the victory the Lord wants for you. Our immediate problems can be physical, emotional, mental, or spiritual; but our ultimate battle is spiritual. Therefore, we must recognize the spiritual aspect of our trials. That means we must understand Satan's role in our struggles.

# CHAPTER TWO

# SATAN'S ROLE IN OUR TRIALS

As one studies the Bible, he is introduced to a wicked fallen angelic being whose name is Lucifer. He has a number of titles which describe his evil ways. He is called the Devil, which means accuser. He is called Satan, which means adversary. He is called the Serpent, which speaks of his deceptive ways. He is called Apollyon, which means destroyer. He is called the Wicked One, which speaks of his evil character. He is the one who "deceiveth the whole world." He is the god of this world, and he hates the true and living God and all who serve Him. He goes about "as a roaring lion seeking whom he may devour." He is your enemy and he wants to devour you. To recognize him and his ways will help you to live victoriously.

The Bible clearly teaches that Satan, our adversary, has a direct role in some of our problems, as he did with Job when he took his health (Job 2:4–8). It is equally clear that he is not the direct cause of every problem. Sometimes he acts against us indirectly by moving men to do evil, as he did in stirring up the Sabeans and Chaldeans against Job (Job 1:10–17). Sometimes he is not personally involved at all. Men have a sinful nature and will do wrong without immediate motivation from the Devil.

Then again, some of our problems are simply part of life in this world. Cars break down, the roof leaks, the pipes break. In time sickness and death come upon all. What we must keep in mind is this—even if Satan is not personally involved in causing our problems, he will seek to use those problems to defeat us spiritually and emotionally. Paul says in II Corinthians 2:11, "We are not ignorant of his (Satan's) devices." In Ephesians 6:10–11 Paul encourages us in our stand against "the wiles (methods) of the Devil," reminding us that "we wrestle not against flesh and blood, but against principalities, against powers, against the rulers of the darkness of this world, against spiritual wickedness in high places." Satan's devices (purposes) and methods of defeating suffering people must be understood or any one of us could become a spiritual casualty. So what are Satan's devices and methods?

### 1. Satan wants to get us to focus on people.

Since we just quoted Ephesians 6:10–11, we should start there. It seems that many of life's troubles involve other people. Personal attack, rumors, lies, misrepresentations, physical harm, and broken promises are but a few of the things people suffer at the hands of others. Of course, if there is physical harm, there may need to be legal or other appropriate action taken against the offender; but Paul wants us to understand that our greatest defeat will not come from what a person says or does to us. It comes when Satan breaks us spiritually, mentally, or emotionally.

When Paul wrote Ephesians, he was in prison, but neither his circumstances nor his human enemies could destroy him. Only if he let Satan steal his peace and joy could Paul fall in defeat. The same is true for you. The people who hurt you are being used by Satan for his purposes. See them as flesh and blood, as weak as or weaker than you. See Satan as the real enemy. When you do, victory will be within reach.

### 2. Satan wants to convince us no one else has suffered as we are suffering.

Satan wants us to fall into a state of self-pity. Elijah was there in I Kings 19. Asaph was there in Psalm 73. Satan wants you to feel so sorry for yourself that you can justify defeat and despair in your life. After all, if no one else has ever been through what you are going through, how can you be expected to have victory? Paul wrote in I Corinthians 10:13, "There hath no temptation taken you but such as is *common to man;* but God is faithful, who will not suffer (allow) you to be tempted above that ye are able; but will with the temptation make a way to escape, that ye may be able to bear it." Others have been through what you are going through and have received victory.

Elijah struggled in great defeat, but Asaph claimed wonderful victory. (Read Psalm 73.) If you want to stay defeated and give Satan the victory, you can choose to be like Elijah. If you refuse to go through life feeling sorry for yourself, victory can be yours like it was for Asaph. These words are not intended to be harsh or reflect a callousness toward your situation. They are important words for each of us. Reflect on them carefully and deeply. Our hurts are real, but we must determine by God's grace that we will claim the victory that the Lord offers us.

### 3. Satan wants to convince us we are at the breaking point.

"I can't take it anymore." How many times I have heard those words and have come close to saying them myself! Let's be careful here. Satan loves to see people quit on the Lord in anger and bitterness. With all Paul went through, he might have felt he could not take it anymore. What an amazing testimony he maintained, however, when he wrote in II Corinthians 4:8–9, "We are troubled on every side, yet not distressed; we are perplexed, but not in despair; persecuted, but not forsaken; cast down, but not destroyed." He obviously also believed what he had written in I Corinthians 10:13, "But God is faithful, *who will not suffer* (allow) *you to be tempted above that ye are able,* but will with the temptation make a way to escape, that ye may be able to bear it." You and I must believe that, too.

This belief did not mean Paul allowed himself to be totally walked over by others. He used legal means to defend himself when he was falsely arrested (Acts 25:10–11), but with all the pressure and conflict that came into his life, he never quit on the Lord and seemingly never lost his joy. Believe this, if you quit on the Lord and abide in anger and bitterness, it is the choice you make and for which you will be responsible. The Lord will *never* allow us to fall into situations where victory is impossible.

### 4. Satan wants to convince us there is no hope.

Despair is one of Satan's greatest weapons against the hurting Christian. Peter writes in I Peter 5:6–11, "Humble yourselves therefore under the mighty hand of God, that he may exalt you in due time: casting all your care upon him; for he careth for you. Be sober, be vigilant; because your adversary the devil, as a roaring lion, walketh about, seeking whom he may devour (drown or swallow): whom resist steadfast in the faith, knowing that the same afflictions are accomplished in your brethren that are in the world. But the

God of all grace, who hath called us unto his eternal glory by Christ Jesus, after that ye have suffered a while, make you perfect, stablish, strengthen, settle you. To him be glory and dominion for ever and ever. Amen."

Peter tells us the Devil, as a roaring lion, is seeking whom he may devour. As noted previously, the term *devour* means to swallow or drown. He wants us to think we are doomed to the sadness and misery we are currently enduring. That may be where you are right now. Peter gives hope by saying, "After ye have suffered a while." The way may seem dark at the moment but, praise the Lord, there is an afterward. Stay strong in faith; God has victory for you. Do not let the Devil devour you.

### 5. *Satan wants to convince us our trouble is the consequence of our sin.*

The more I read and study the Bible, the more I stand in awe of the mercy and grace of God. We deserve the consequence of sin, and the Bible tells us clearly, "As we sow, so shall we reap." At the same time a review of all the people we listed in the first chapter of this book will reveal that very few of them suffered as a direct consequence of sin, but it does happen. Achan died directly because of sin (Joshua 7:1–26). Paul told the church at Corinth that their sin had caused some to be sick and others to die (I Corinthians 11:29–31). So if you believe your suffering is due to sin in your life, do not give up. Do what the Bible says. Get down on your knees and confess your sin to the Lord. When you do, John says in I John 1:9, "He (God) is faithful and just to forgive us our sins, and to cleanse us from all unrighteousness." Determine that with the Lord's help you will forsake the sin and not do it again.

You cannot change what you did, and there may be consequences you must bear because of it, but do not continue to carry the burden of it. If you have every reason to believe your suffering is due to your own sin, be willing to accept those consequences from the hand of the Lord, but do not spend the rest of your life in spiritual and emotional defeat. The Devil would love to have you live the rest of your life carrying a load of guilt.

If your sin was against someone else, you need to try to make things right with them. The Lord wants to forgive. Accept God's forgiveness and let Him set you free. He is truly a God of new beginnings. You can have a fresh start before the Lord.

At the same time, realize that many troublesome situations are not the direct result of sin. The Lord may be allowing a trial of your faith through which He wants you to grow spiritually and learn lessons you could learn in no other way.

### 6. Satan wants to defeat us through bitterness.

Bitterness is associated with hurt and is rooted in pride. The solution to bitterness toward people is forgiveness. We will take this up in more detail later, but remember this: God resists the proud.

Pride was Satan's sin (I Timothy 3:6). Pride is to think of ourselves more highly than we ought to think (Romans 12:3). We can get bitter when someone has done or said something toward us that we think was wrong, unfair, or unjust. God tells us how to handle such offenses, but too often pride takes over creating a haughty spirit and a high-minded attitude. The results are devastating.

When we grieve the Holy Spirit (Ephesians 4:30), God resists (opposes) us (James 4:6) and we are left troubled, while creating defilement in others (Hebrews 12:15). When we get in a state of bitterness, we are poisoned by it and we are exactly where the Devil wants us. No one finds it easy to admit they are bitter, but the Bible says in Proverbs 14:10, "The heart knoweth his own bitterness." If you are bitter, you know it. Don't stay there—it will ruin your life.

### 7. Satan wants us to doubt God's love.

"Why would a loving God _____?" You can fill in the blank. The question has been asked thousands of times. The answer I have had to give many times is "I do not know why God allowed this situation, but this I do know..." From that point on I have sought to explain these foundational truths.

· Genesis 18:25 — "Shall not the Judge of all the earth do right?" Abraham spoke these words, not to express doubt about God, but to remind himself that God always does right.

· Romans 8:38–39 — "For I am persuaded, that neither death, nor life, nor angels, nor principalities, nor powers, nor things present, nor things to come, nor height, nor depth, nor any other creature, shall be able to separate us from the love of God, which is in Christ Jesus our Lord." We need never doubt God's love because nothing can move us outside the realm of His loving care.

· Romans 8:28 — "And we know that all things work together for good to them that love God, to them who are the called according to his purpose." Not only does God love us, He also includes us in the workings of His eternal purpose.

There is a spiritual reason for everything God does or allows in our lives. The issue is never whether God loves us—He does! In our finite minds we cannot always comprehend what He is doing or why He is doing it, but we can rest in the truths reflected in the verses quoted above.

### 8. Satan wants us to question God's Word.

Satan has from the beginning of time attacked the integrity of God by causing people to question His Word. In Genesis 3:1–4 it all started with the temptation of Adam and Eve. Satan called into question what God said and then directly called God a liar. He wanted them to believe they could not trust the spoken Word of God. He wants us to believe we cannot trust the Bible—the written Word of God. He wants us to doubt that the Bible is God's Word, and he wants to convince us that we cannot trust its message and promises.

The Lord Jesus prayed for us in John 17:17, "Sanctify them (us) through thy truth: thy word is truth." The Psalmist wrote in Psalm 119:89 & 105, "For ever, O Lord, thy word is settled in heaven…Thy word is a lamp unto my feet, and a light unto my path." If Satan can get you to doubt the Word of God, he will take away any chance for you to ever get victory.

### 9. Satan wants to make us think God should have given us a better life.

Satan sought to undermine Adam and Eve's trust in God by telling them they deserved better than God gave them and, in fact, that He intentionally refused to give them the best. God warned Adam and Eve to not eat the fruit of the tree of the knowledge of good and evil because when they did they would die. Satan called God a liar. He then told Adam and Eve that God knew if they ate the fruit they would be like God and God did not want them to have that privilege (Genesis 3:4–5).

How wonderful the promise of Psalm 84:11, "No good thing will he withhold from them that walk uprightly." So many people think they have been robbed or cheated out of life's best. They believe life has treated them unfairly and God is ultimately responsible. God tried to protect Adam and Eve from things He saw that they could not see. Thinking God had been unfair, they plunged into sin and death. You can trust God! He knows what is best for you and will not withhold from you any good thing.

Has Satan defeated you through his methods and wicked devices? He is a master at destroying people. Before we take up consideration of how to get victory over our trials, let's see what the Bible tells us about God's role in our suffering.

# CHAPTER THREE
# GOD'S ROLE IN OUR SUFFERING

Where is God to be found in our experience of trial and suffering? Praise the Lord, He is near. Paul wrote in Philippians 4:5, "The Lord is at hand." The Psalmist wrote in Psalm 46:1, "God is...a very present help in trouble." We must accept the truth that the Lord does not promise us a life without trouble. In fact, He tells us over and over again that we will have problems. Eliphaz did not get everything right, but he is on target when he says in Job 5:7, "Yet man is born unto trouble, as the sparks fly upward." Job himself says in Job 14:1, "Man that is born of a woman is of few days, and full of trouble." In John 16:33 our Lord Jesus says, "In the world ye shall have tribulation." God does not promise us a life without trial, but His promises are rich with hope. He will walk with us through every experience. Consider some of the specific truths regarding the Lord's role in our hard times.

### 1. God allows suffering, but always for a special purpose.

Reading the book of Job opens our understanding regarding some of our suffering. Satan wanted to cause problems for Job and would have killed him, if Satan had his way. But Satan could go no further than God allowed (Job 1:12 & 2:6). Thank the Lord today—you are not at the mercy of the Devil, for he has no mercy. You are in God's hands. Yes, He has allowed the suffering, but never for the purpose of seeing you defeated or destroyed.

· Asaph was almost in total defeat before he found victory, but once he renewed his spiritual perspective, he could say in Psalm 73:1, "Truly God is good to Israel, even to such as are of a clean heart."

· While our situations pale in significance to those of the Lord Jesus, we can pray as He did in Matthew 26:39, "O my Father, if it be possible, let this cup pass from me: nevertheless not as I will, but as thou wilt." There was a divine purpose in the suffering of the Lord and there is a divine purpose in what you and I go through.

When we pull back from the emotion of our hardship, we can rest in the certainty that, if there was no divine purpose, God would not have allowed our suffering to occur. He allows our suffering because there is divine purpose that requires it. Job could not grasp God's purpose in his trial, but he rested in it. He says in Job 23:10, "But he knoweth the way that I take: when he hath tried me, I shall come forth as gold." You may not see God's purpose right now, but rest in the fact that there is one. By God's grace, you too shall come forth as gold.

### 2. God carries us through our trials.

Isaiah 46:3–4 was spoken to Israel, but it is applicable to you and me. Meditate on these words. "Hearken unto me, O house of Jacob, and all the remnant of the house of Israel, which are borne by me from the belly, which are carried from the womb; and even to your old age I am he; and even to hoar hairs will I carry you: I have made, and I will bear; even I will carry, and will deliver you."

Right now, God is carrying you. You could not make it any other way. You may feel totally defeated and convinced you cannot go on. By God's grace you go on because you are not dependent on your own strength, wisdom, or ability.

Peter speaks these words of comfort and assurance in I Peter 5:7, "Casting all your care upon him; for he careth for (takes care of) you." The Lord never planned the Christian life to be lived in the strength of the Christian. Cast yourself on the Lord. He is there for you. David wrote in Psalm 37:23–24, "The steps of a good man are ordered by the Lord: and he delighteth in his way. Though he fall, he shall not be utterly cast down: for the Lord upholdeth him with his hand."

### 3. God gives grace to handle our suffering.

In II Corinthians 12:1–10 Paul gives testimony about his suffering. He was attacked by Satan with what he called a thorn in the flesh. No one knows exactly what it was, but Paul besought the Lord three times that it might depart from him. God did not give him his desire but answered with these words, "My grace is sufficient for thee: for my strength is made perfect in weakness." In other words, the Lord told Paul that He would enable him to bear the suffering. He said that Paul would see that in his own weakness (lack of strength) God's power would be sufficient.

Sometimes our suffering is not brought to an end as we would desire. We think we could get victory if only our circumstances would change. The Lord wanted Paul, and us, to know that even when difficult circumstances continue we can still have victory by the grace and power of God.

The word *sufficient* means enough. It speaks of gaining strength and finding contentment. The promise of sufficiency was God's way of telling Paul he could find contentment and live victoriously in spite of his ongoing suffering. So sufficient was God's grace that Paul could say in verse 9, "Most gladly therefore will I rather glory in my infirmities, that the power of Christ may rest upon me." In other words, Paul found such peace in the grace of God that he no longer felt the need to ask that his circumstances be changed. The depth of God's grace is something that few ever experience, but it is available to you.

### 4. God is always present with us in trial and suffering.

We have already mentioned Psalm 46:1, but let's emphasize it here. It says, "God is our refuge and strength, a very present help in trouble." Paul told Timothy in II Timothy 4:16–17, "At my first answer no man stood with me, but all men forsook me:...Notwithstanding the Lord stood with me, and strengthened me." What a wonderful testimony! Hebrews 13:5–6 says, "He hath said, I will never leave thee nor forsake thee, so that we may boldly say,...I will not fear what man shall do unto me."

The only recorded instance of God ever forsaking any of His own was when He forsook the Lord Jesus Christ on the cross. Our Savior cried out, "My God, my God, why hast thou forsaken me?" (Matthew 27:46) Yes, the Father forsook His Son at Calvary as He bore the sins of the world and became a curse for us—but your heavenly Father will never forsake you. Psalm 34:7 says, "The angel of the Lord encampeth round about them that fear him, and delivereth them."

## 5. God gives peace which passes understanding.

In Philippians 4:6–7 the Lord offers peace that passes understanding. There are conditions that must be met for us to receive that peace, but it is available. Peace—that quiet condition of the heart when we are resting in the Lord and finding contentment within, though there is turmoil all about us.

The term *peace* means to be joined or at one again. When there is division between people, we can easily understand the term, but Philippians is talking about peace within. When trouble comes we can be double-minded, not knowing what to do. Our minds can be racing with confusing thoughts. Peace settles the racing mind and restores the ability to think with quietness and clarity. What a wonderful gift God offers us in the time of trouble! You can have the peace that passes understanding. It comes from the Lord and only from Him.

## 6. God promises the ultimate victory.

There is a great day coming. It will be the day when the Lord makes everything right. The Apostle Paul speaks of *that day* in II Timothy 1:12, 1:18, and 4:8. He has the same thought in mind when he says in I Corinthians 4:5, "[The Lord] will bring to light the hidden things of darkness,…then shall every man have praise of God." What a day it will be when "God shall wipe away all tears from their eyes; and there shall be no more death, neither sorrow, nor crying, neither shall there be any more pain: for the former things are passed away" (Revelation 21:4). Paul tells us in Romans 8:18 that "the sufferings of this present time are not worthy to be compared with the glory which shall be revealed in us."

A great part of God's role in our suffering is the promise of future and permanent peace and joy. Don't quit!

# CHAPTER FOUR

# PAUL'S PERSONAL TESTIMONY OF VICTORY

There are a number of passages in the Bible that might be called victory passages. Some of these texts were given specifically to teach us how to respond to trials, while others relate actual experiences of believers to show us how they responded to trials. There are more than we will be able to examine in this text, but we will open up enough of them so you will be able to claim the victory the Lord has for you. In the text before us, the Apostle Paul will tell us of his personal victory over trial, and, as an added blessing, he will tell us how he got that victory.

## II Corinthians 4:7–18

7 *But we have this treasure in earthen vessels, that the excellency of the power may be of God, and not of us.*

8 *We are troubled on every side, yet not distressed; we are perplexed, but not in despair;*

9 *Persecuted, but not forsaken; cast down, but not destroyed;*

10 *Always bearing about in the body the dying of the Lord Jesus, that the life also of Jesus might be made manifest in our body.*

11 *For we which live are alway delivered unto death for Jesus' sake, that the life also of Jesus might be made manifest in our mortal flesh.*

12 *So then death worketh in us, but life in you.*

13 *We having the same spirit of faith, according as it is written, I believed,*

*and therefore have I spoken; we also believe, and therefore speak;*

*[14] Knowing that he which raised up the Lord Jesus shall raise up us also by Jesus, and shall present us with you.*

*[15] For all things are for your sakes, that the abundant grace might through the thanksgiving of many redound to the glory of God.*

*[16] For which cause we faint not; but though our outward man perish, yet the inward man is renewed day by day.*

*[17] For our light affliction, which is but for a moment, worketh for us a far more exceeding and eternal weight of glory;*

*[18] While we look not at the things which are seen, but at the things which are not seen: for the things which are seen are temporal; but the things which are not seen are eternal.*

This passage of Scripture is a testimony of the Apostle Paul and is given to the believers of Corinth to encourage them in their times of trial and difficulty. Follow its message carefully.

In verse 7 Paul talks about having a treasure in an earthen vessel. The treasure is the wonderful truth of the Gospel of the Lord Jesus Christ. Paul reminds his readers, however, of the frailty of those, including himself, who carry the gospel message. He does this by referring to himself as an "earthen vessel." Earthen vessels are made of clay and are easily broken. How weak and subject to breaking are we? Though Paul was a preacher of the greatest truth in the world (the treasure), he himself (the earthen vessel) was weak and subject to many kinds of testing and suffering. His point is so good for us to consider. You and I are weak. How easily we can be hurt or injured physically, emotionally, or spiritually. We, too, are earthen vessels, so easily broken.

Paul tells us of his struggles in life as well as the victory he enjoyed in spite of them. In verses 8–10 he tells about his difficult circumstances. Maybe you can relate to them. He says, "We are troubled on every side,… we are perplexed,…persecuted,…cast down,…always bearing about in the body the dying of the Lord Jesus." Are you in there?

The term *troubled* means to be pressured and afflicted, and Paul felt it from *every* side. Everywhere he turned there were problems. For you, that same kind of situation could mean difficulties with job, family, finances, or physical ailment. Sometimes it seems we have problems wherever we turn. Then Paul says he was *perplexed.* That meant he did not know what to do. We can be just like that. The difficulties of life seem overwhelming, and we do not know what to do to solve our problems. Paul also says he was *persecuted* which for him was for the sake of the gospel. Perhaps you feel persecuted. It may not be strictly for preaching the gospel. Maybe it has to do with standing for what is right when others do not seem to care. But for whatever reason, you may feel the heartache of rejection by others.

Next, Paul says he was *cast down.* The term *cast down* suggests that no matter what Paul tried to do to relieve his difficulty nothing worked. His efforts had been defeated. His enemies seemed to have victory. He says he was "always bearing about in [his] body the dying" of Jesus Christ. In other words, he was constantly suffering for and in the name of the Lord Jesus.

Question—Can you identify with Paul's problems? But wait! Can you identify with Paul's spiritual victory as readily as you might identify with his afflictions? Look at the full picture. Paul says he was troubled, ***but not distressed.*** To be *distressed* means to be so pressured that you are paralyzed, unable to move because of the burden. He says he was perplexed, ***but not in despair.*** Paul did not know what to do, but he had not lost hope. His hope was in the Lord, and he knew, in due time, that the Lord would guide him in making whatever decisions were before him. He says he was persecuted, ***but not forsaken.*** He was continually aware of the comforting presence of the Lord, in spite of those who were acting against him. He says he was cast down, ***but not destroyed.*** Down, but not out. He was dying in body, but he grasped the truth that the purpose of his suffering was to manifest the life and power of the Lord Jesus in his life. He was an earthen vessel, but he was indwelt and empowered by the living Christ. Oh, sweet victory! I want it, too!

What is it that brought such wonderful victory to Paul in the face of terrible trial? Thankfully, he tells us so we can get victory, too. In verse 13 he quotes to us from Psalm 116:10 which says, "I believed, therefore have I spoken." I encourage you to stop and read that whole psalm. It sets the stage for what Paul is going to say in the rest of his message to the Corinthians. The psalmist tells of his suffering, defeat, and fear. He says the sorrows of death had compassed him. He found trouble and sorrow, but then he tells how he cried to the Lord and was delivered. He acknowledges the Lord to be gracious, righteous, and merciful. He encourages his own soul to return to rest because the Lord "delivered my soul from death, mine eyes from tears, and my feet from falling" (Psalm 116:8).

After quoting the psalmist, Paul unveils the pathway to that same kind of spiritual success in his own life and for us. Here is what worked for him and what will work for you and me. He starts in II Corinthians 4:14 by recalling the ultimate victory that will someday come. "He which raised up the Lord Jesus shall raise up us." Paul knew that heaven was real and the day was coming when all sorrow would end. This blessed assurance was the foundation of his victory.

> *We tend to think things happen TO us rather than FOR us.*

It is no wonder that those who have never come to Christ are falling apart. They turn to psychiatrists and psychologists; they try drugs; they drink to forget; they sometimes take their own lives. Why? Because underneath their troubled lives, there is no hope. Paul had hope in Christ. If you are saved, you do too. Rejoicing and reveling in that hope will diminish the pain of the present. I guarantee it—because that is what the Bible teaches. Our eternal hope in Christ is an anchor for our soul. The day will come when sorrow and trouble will be no more. However, Paul wants us to know there is victory available to us in the here and now. Let's claim it.

After reminding us of the resurrection that awaits us, Paul focuses on the divine purpose for suffering in this life. In verse 15 he tells the believers at Corinth, "For all things are for your sakes." I remember when this truth was first brought home to my heart through the ministry of a dear servant of the Lord, Dr. George Mundell. From time to time during my pastoral ministry I asked Dr. Mundell to come preach Spiritual Life Conferences. Along with other precious truths, he often reminded us that "all things are for your sakes." We tend to think things happen *TO* us, but this Scripture teaches that things happen *FOR* us.

Did you get that truth? If I could talk to you today and you could share with me your story, you might tell me of the many things that have happened *to* you. Paul says we must grasp that the experiences of life do not happen *to* us. They happen *for* us. If we go through life focusing on all the things that have happened to us, we will develop a victim mentality. We will tend to feel sorry for ourselves. If we see that things happen *for* us, we can look for the Lord in every situation. Through every experience He is at work in our lives seeking to deepen our faith. In everything we go through or witness in the lives of others, all of it is for our sake. There is a divine purpose in everything. Faith can be deepened; lessons can be learned; strength can be gained. Paul understood it for himself and he wanted the believers at Corinth to grasp it, too. Don't miss the tender opportunity of asking the Lord to help you experience the fulfillment of His purpose in your trial. Do not let your heartache be in vain. Ask the Lord to begin to open your mind and heart to what the Lord intended *for* you through the trial you are facing today.

Paul then introduces the abundant grace of God, which he says will *redound* (produce abundantly) to the glory of God. Paul knew of God's grace in his own life. It had been sufficient to provide emotional and spiritual security in times past, and it would be enough this time. He also knew that when others saw the sufficiency of God's grace in his life they would be moved to glorify God. Nothing was more important to Paul than that. If in your discouragement you have lost sight of seeking to glorify God, pray and ask Him to help you in your trial that He may be glorified through your victory.

In the middle of verse 15 Paul put his finger on the proverbial "key that unlocks the door" to God's grace. This is a truth that few understand. It is stated often in the Word, but it is beyond us humanly so we ignore it or reject it. Thanksgiving! Paul in his situation and the believers at Corinth in their situations had to come to the place of thanking the Lord for what they were going through. Have you done that yet? It follows perfectly with Paul's teaching. If all things are for our sakes, should we not thank God for them? If there is divine purpose being worked out in our experiences, should we not thank God for it? Don't balk at this challenge. Seek to grasp its significance.

Thanking the Lord for what has happened in your life is not an appeal to emotion. The challenge is not to *feel* thankful. The challenge is to *give thanks*. It is okay to say, "Lord, I do not feel thankful. I am hurting. I am angry at people. I do not understand why you would have let this happen. BUT, in obedience to your Word, by faith I thank you for what has happened." In some ways giving thanks is the hardest message I preach from a pulpit or give in counsel, but it is right. When you give thanks, you acknowledge there is divine purpose—God has not deserted you. He is involved, and, equally important, your expression of thanks by faith opens the door to God's abundant grace being poured out to you. When you thank Him, you are humbling yourself before Him. We will discuss this challenge again in Chapter 5.

Now, we move to verse 16. Paul tells of the victory he is enjoying. He says, "For which cause we faint not." To *faint not* means Paul had not lost courage to go on; he had not lost his heart for the battle. Humanly, he had every justification to give up, but he did not. The reason was the sustaining grace of God. When he says "for which cause," he was referring to God's grace. God's grace caused him to keep on going. He goes on to say, "Though the outward man perish, yet the inward man is renewed day by day." Paul's testimony was clear. Even if things continued to go wrong outwardly (physically and circumstantially), he was experiencing daily renewal of strength in the inward man. His external problems were not weakening him within.

How often the outward things finally *get to us*. We give up, collapse under the pressure, say things we should not say. We just do not care anymore. When that kind of thing happens, it is evidence that we are handling the problems on our own and we are failing. The "earthen vessel" has cracked. For Paul the outward man was wearing down and eventually would wear out, but not the inner man. The inner man was being sustained by God's grace. It was being renewed day by day. One day at a time Paul was finding everything he needed to go on victoriously. You and I have the same opportunity for victory that was available to Paul.

In verses 17 and 18 Paul reminds us again of the importance of that eternal perspective he mentioned in verse 14. He acknowledges in verse 17 that the problems on this earth will pale into insignificance when we are finally with the Lord. That is going to happen for all of us. But there was a practical side of that eternal perspective. He not only had hope for heaven, but he daily refused discouragement. He says in verse 18, "We look not at the things which are seen." To *look* means to give consideration or to take heed. Paul knew he could get discouraged if he continually dwelt on his trials. The same is true for us. If, when things go wrong, all we do is focus on them and think about them, we are doomed. Paul did not hide his head in the sand and just hope everything would go away, but he was not going to dwell on the negatives 24 hours a day. Instead, Paul focused on the spiritual and eternal truths of God's Word.

This world is not home for us. The heartaches here will someday be swallowed up in eternal victory. The psalmist wrote in Psalm 127:2, "It is vain for you to rise up early, to sit up late, to eat the bread of sorrows: for so he giveth his beloved sleep." Paul got that message. We must get it, too. No one is exempt from trouble, not even Paul, a wonderful servant of Christ; however, trouble does not necessarily lead to distress, despair, and destruction. It is not what happens to us; it is how we respond to it. The victory that came to Paul will be ours when we respond as he responded.

We started our investigation of victory passages with II Corinthians 4:7–18 because the testimony comes out of Paul's personal experience. He was not a classroom instructor giving theory about victory over trial. He was hurting as much as you or I hurt, but he had a story to tell about the grace of God in his life. We need it! We need to believe what he believed and do what he did.

# CHAPTER FIVE

# FIRST STEP TOWARD VICTORY

There is perhaps no greater challenge to us when we are hurting than the exhortation to give thanks. Humanly, it does not make sense. It is, however, an act of faith and humility. It is submitting to God when we want to the least. It is casting ourselves on Him when we want to demand answers as to why the trouble has been allowed to come. Consider the Lord's instruction in this area.

I Thessalonians 5:18 says, "In every thing give thanks: for this is the will of God in Christ Jesus concerning you." We need to address this text and ones with a similar challenge early in our examination of the victory passages. We saw reference to *thanksgiving* in II Corinthians 4:15 and we will see it again. But I Thessalonians 5:18 is a direct instruction to which we must give heed. Let's look at it.

"In every thing" conveys the idea of every matter and every condition. It is not teaching, as some suggest, that in bad times we should look for the redeeming aspects of the situation. Some would render the verse as "In the midst of everything, give thanks." For instance, I have heard some teach that this passage might be used when someone breaks a leg. The interpretation is that we should give thanks that we did not break both legs. But that is not the scriptural challenge. "Lord, I thank you for my broken leg" would be in harmony with the biblical teaching. We may not know why the Lord allowed it and we may not see the benefit of it, but we rest in the truth that God's ways are not our ways and are surely above our ways. He had a purpose in allowing that leg to be broken.

We believe Romans 8:28 and can apply it to the most mundane of life's experiences. "And we know that *all things* work together for good to them who are the called according to his purpose." It is the truth of

Romans 8:28 that enables us to give thanks. The hurts in life are real, but our God is great enough to work those hurtful experiences to produce good. In fact, the good things God will bring out of that bad circumstance may come in no other way. In pure human experience, imagine you are driving down the road and have a flat tire. Someone stops to help, and you develop a lasting friendship with the one who helped you. Out of the bad experience, a dear and lasting friendship was created. This is a trite example, but it illustrates in a simple way what the wonderful God of heaven can do, for the sake of eternity, through the hard times of our lives.

I Thessalonians 5:18 goes on, "For this is the will of God." This phrase tells us that God *wills* us to give thanks. It is not a suggestion, it is an expectation. It is God's will concerning us who are in Christ Jesus. The word *concerning* is a preposition that conveys intent or purpose. When the verse says, "This is the will of God…concerning you," it means intended or purposed for you. This verse tells us that it is the Lord's intention and purpose for us, in every matter or circumstance, to give thanks.

I want to emphasize that this instruction is for the believer, the one who is *in* Christ Jesus. In the same way, Romans 8:28 is for the believer, "…them who are the called according to his purpose." The unbeliever is outside the intimate workings of God, which He has reserved for His children. While discouraged believers often feel forsaken by the Lord, the very opposite is true. You may not understand what the Lord is doing in your life, but you can trust Him. Thank Him now for the difficult situation you may be facing or the hard trial you have come through.

Ephesians 5:4 calls for the "giving of thanks." In the earlier verses of the chapter, Paul reminds us of Christ's love for us and that He gave Himself for us as an offering to God. He challenges us to refuse sinful living and to choose rather the giving of thanks.

In Ephesians 5:20 the exhortation is "giving thanks always for all things unto God." These words are given in conjunction with the instruction to be filled with the Holy Spirit found in Ephesians 5:18. One evidence of being filled with the Spirit is that we will be able to give "thanks always for all things." In ourselves we cannot do that. We can give thanks for good things, and we can usually give thanks that things are not worse. Who can give thanks for *all* things? We have already seen Paul's testimony in II Corinthians 4. The "thanksgiving of many" was possible through the recognition that "all things are for our sakes." Paul, no doubt, had an awareness of that truth, as he calls for us to give thanks for all things in Ephesians 5:20.

These challenges are not ignored in Paul's Colossian letter. In Colossians 2:7, Paul is discussing our salvation in Christ and that we are to be "stablished in the faith...abounding therein with thanksgiving." These encouragements are given while Paul acknowledges that these believers will face many obstacles as they seek to live for the Lord. In Colossians 3:15 the exhortation "be ye thankful" is included with instructions for godly living. In Colossians 4:2 "watch in the same with thanksgiving" is a directive concerning the believer's prayer life. You will find more texts on thanksgiving if you take time to search.

If you still have not thanked the Lord for what has happened in your life, do it now. I mean right now before you read another sentence. Remember, it is not an appeal to your emotions. Many things will occur for which we will not feel thankful. It is an appeal to our faith. God has allowed this hurt for a purpose. He can take it and use it for His glory and our spiritual good. If we shut ourselves away from the Lord, the hurt will be in vain. If trouble must come, let the Lord use it to produce spiritual benefit in our lives.

*The hurts in life are real, but our God is great enough to work those hurtful experiences to produce good.*

Sometimes I read statements or phrases in Scripture and wonder if I can even come close to grasping the depth of them. These challenges to give thanks fall into that category. I have not had near the trials in my life that some of my dearest friends and loved ones have faced. In my trials, however, I have sought to develop a readiness to give thanks to God as an initial response to the difficulty. It has helped me to get a better perspective on the situation and helped me to immediately start looking for the hand of the Lord at work. I have seen others who have gone through far greater trial do the same. When expressions of thanks flow from our lips, we glorify God and we open ourselves to another work of His grace in our lives.

I do not share these thoughts lightly, as if the heartaches of life are easy to bear. I have seen the deepest of trials in the lives of those in my church and in the experiences of friends. Trouble respects no one, and it comes in many forms. A danger for us is to think that our trouble may somehow be outside of this biblical challenge. You may have been deeply hurt through abuse, attack, or disease. You may think it would be easy to thank God for the broken leg in our illustration, but it would be impossible to thank God for what you have gone through or what you may be facing now or in the future.

I can well remember one lady who wondered how thanking God for her situation could even be brought up. There were anger and tears at the very mention of such an idea. The only way victory came for her was when she began to look for the good things that came out of her trouble and other good things that could still come. As she considered them, the Lord graciously gave her a taste of His ability and intent to work that tragedy for good. The Lord gave her a wonderful victory.

The Apostle Paul gained such amazing victory in his troubles that he could write in II Corinthians 12:10, "Therefore I *take pleasure* in infirmities, in reproaches, in necessities, in persecutions, in distresses for Christ's sake: for when I am weak, then am I strong." I can read that text and know I am not there. I do not think the lady I just referred to is there. You may never get there either; but by faith, we can all say, "Lord, I give you thanks." Then we can beg God for grace, strength, peace, and victory. It may be through tears, but I encourage you to bow your heart before the Lord right now. By faith, give thanks for your trial.

# CHAPTER SIX

# Peace That Passeth Understanding

*Philippians 4:4–9*

<sup>4</sup> *Rejoice in the Lord alway: and again I say, Rejoice.*

<sup>5</sup> *Let your moderation be known unto all men. The Lord is at hand.*

<sup>6</sup> *Be careful for nothing; but in every thing by prayer and supplication with thanksgiving let your requests be made known unto God.*

<sup>7</sup> *And the peace of God, which passeth all understanding, shall keep your hearts and minds through Christ Jesus.*

<sup>8</sup> *Finally, brethren, whatsoever things are true, whatsoever things are honest, whatsoever things are just, whatsoever things are pure, whatsoever things are lovely, whatsoever things are of good report; if there be any virtue, and if there be any praise, think on these things.*

<sup>9</sup> *Those things, which ye have both learned, and received, and heard, and seen in me, do: and the God of peace shall be with you.*

Do you want peace? Here is another text from the Word of God which is filled with hope and encouragement for us. Verses 4 and 5 call for us to have a proper perspective on life. Paul begins by telling us to "rejoice in the Lord." We tend to rejoice in what the Lord does for us rather than to rejoice *in Him*.

A great part of the testing experience in Job's life was to prove why he worshipped the Lord. Satan said in Job 1:9, "Doth Job fear God for nought?" He went on to announce to God that the only reason Job served God was because of the rich blessings God had given him. He told God that if the physical, family, and financial prosperity was taken away Job would curse God to His face. When all was said and done, it turned out that Job served God because He was God, not because of the blessings. The challenge is the same for us in Philippians. Rejoice in the Lord! Is your joy found in the Lord, or is your joy found only in what the Lord does for you?

In Nehemiah 8:10, Nehemiah told the people of Israel, "Neither be ye sorry; for the joy of the Lord is your strength." If you are hurting in some way right now, it is not easy to rejoice in anything, but this is a time to turn to the Lord. Thank Him for your salvation. Thank Him for His love and compassion. Thank Him that someday the Lord Jesus is coming again. Thank Him for His faithfulness and that He does not change. You may not find much in your circumstances to produce joy, but you can rejoice in the Lord.

Paul goes on to say, "Let your moderation be known unto all men. The Lord is at hand." The term translated *moderation* in our Bible could be translated patience, forbearance, or gentleness. It is an attitude of self control, spiritual steadfastness, and emotional stability that maintains a strong testimony for the Lord, even in hard times. It is in contrast to being contentious. We are enabled to exhibit moderation because, as Paul goes on to remind us, "the Lord is at hand." While this is a reminder that He is coming again, it is primarily a reminder of His presence with us. He has not forsaken us. He is nearby.

At the very beginning of this book, we pointed out that the greatest test during trial is not what we go through but how we respond to it. If we respond incorrectly to bad situations or offensive people, we only complicate the matter. The Lord is hindered from helping us, Satan gets his way, and our defeat is all the greater. We must not react impulsively or contentiously in a trying time. We need to be patient, forbearing, and gentle. We can do that if we step back and look for the Lord. He is at hand. He is near. We are in a spiritual battle and we must fight in a spiritual way. Paul teaches us to focus on the Lord, to rejoice in Him, to find comfort in His presence, and to respond in moderation to our difficulties. A further response is called for in the next verse.

Verse 6 is one of the best known texts in the Bible, and it is important for us to consider it. It starts with the exhortation to "be careful for nothing." To *be careful* means to take thought or be anxious. It suggests fretting and worrying. The term itself suggests the danger of getting so concerned about a matter that it distracts us from other things that need our attention. Are you so upset and worried that you cannot think straight? Are you so taken up with your trouble that you are being consumed by it? The Bible says you must stop! Easier said than done, but the Lord tells us what to do.

He says "in everything" (which includes what you are facing today) we are to let our requests "be made known unto God." Our requests are our petitions. We should ask God to solve our problems and minister to our hearts. He already knows what we are going to request, but He wants us to ask. He says we should ask by "prayer and supplication." Prayer is the common idea of praying. Supplication is a stronger word that means to beg, out of need. Usually people worry *or* pray. People who worry to distraction seldom pray; people who pray seldom worry. If you are not begging God to work in you and your situation, start right now. Christians typically say they are going to pray for someone or pray about a situation, but really do very little fervent praying. Start praying about your difficulties and tell the Lord what you would like Him to do.

Right in the midst of the challenge to pray, Paul brings up a truth we have already discussed. The prayer and supplication is to be made "with thanksgiving." Have you thanked the Lord for the trial yet? You must, even if it is with tears. We saw in II Corinthians 4:15 that giving thanks opens the door to God's all sufficient grace. In I Thessalonians 5:18 we saw that giving thanks is God's intention and purpose for us in every situation. In Philippians 4:7 we find that giving thanks opens the door to the peace that passes understanding. We cannot live victoriously without peace, and we cannot have peace in the midst of trial without giving thanks.

Verse 7 brings the promise of peace, and what a peace it is! It brings such quietude of mind and spirit that it is beyond our human comprehension. Notice this important fact. This verse does not promise a change in circumstances; it promises a change in us. Many people do not believe peace and victory can come until circumstances change. Remember, some circumstances will not change, but victory is available. The promise of peace is conditioned upon the believer following the instructions of verse 6. When we do, we get the peace of God that passes (surpasses, is far above) all understanding (our ability to perceive or grasp).

Peace, as we have seen earlier, is a quietness and contentment in the midst of turmoil. This peace will *keep* our hearts and minds. Think about this—because it is extremely important. This term translated *keep* is a military term that means "to guard or protect." During times of trial our hearts and minds need to be protected because they are vulnerable. In times of trouble the unguarded heart can become hardened, wounded, and bitter. Many people have been negatively affected for their whole lives because they never got over the hurts that life brought them. Some live in a shell where they stay to themselves. They withhold their love from others. They don't get involved with people or the service of the Lord because they do not want to risk getting hurt again. Oh, how our hearts need the protective care of God's perfect peace in troublesome circumstances. Not only does that peace guard our hearts, but it also guards our minds. Why do so many people have mind (mental) problems and breakdowns? It is because they have been overcome by their troubles. They are driven to distraction. They cannot handle pressures and soon give up, unable to carry on life's struggles for another day. The Lord tells us there is a peace available to us that will protect our minds from such destruction. It is offered graciously to the child of God. Yes, as already noted, it is the peace that passes understanding.

There is further responsibility for the believer, however, and we must not ignore it. In verse 8 Paul tells us to take charge of our thinking. Thinking can be wonderful as we plan, imagine, and dream of good things in the future or as we reflect upon special times of the past. Thinking can also be destructive and defeating. The Apostle tells us in verse 8 what to think about and what not to think about, especially in hard times. He gives a list and then he qualifies it for us. He says to think on the things that are true, honest, just, pure, lovely, and of good report. A brief commentary on each term may help here.

- *True* speaks of things that are true and factual. Do not give thought to rumors, lies, half truths, etc.

- *Honest* speaks of honorable things and things that inspire reverence and awe, as opposed to those things that are negative and worthless.

- *Just* speaks of things that are right. If we were speaking of actions and told someone to "do the right thing," they would know what we meant. In this context Paul is discussing thinking. He says that in every situation we are to think the *right* thing.

- *Pure* speaks of that which is free from defilement and contamination. Our thinking should be morally clean.

· *Lovely* speaks of that which is loving and friendly toward people.

· *Of good report* speaks of things that enhance others in our minds. Are there some people of whom you can only think negatively? If so, maybe you better not think of them at all until you get control of your thinking.

The Apostle not only gives us a list to guide our thinking, but also qualifies that list by saying, "if there be any virtue, and if there be any praise." *Virtue* implies moral excellence and *praise* denotes that which brings honor to God or commendation to people. As we said, these two terms are qualifiers for thinking. For instance, Paul told us to think on the true and factual. However, in a particular instance the true and factual information regarding some circumstances may not be morally excellent, nor will thoughts about those things bring praise to God or commendation to others. If such is the case, we must not think about it even though it is true.

The thought life is a battleground for all of us. Too many people are victims of their own thinking. They begin to think about something hurtful, wicked, or worrisome, and then they let their thoughts run away with them. They experience terrible mental and emotional defeat. Is that where you are? The Lord tells us we must take charge of our thought life. If you have gotten into the habit of uncontrolled, negative, and ungodly thinking patterns, now is the time to begin anew. It will not be easy, but victory is essential for continuing spiritual, mental, and emotional well-being.

In verse 9 Paul gives us one further instruction. DO! Do what? For the Philippians it was the things they had learned, received, heard, and seen in the life of the Apostle himself. Paul had shown them how to live and now he told them to do as he had done. Sometimes we do not know the right thing to do. Paul expressed that in his own life in II Corinthians 4:8 when he said he was perplexed. If right now you are perplexed and do not know what to do, then wait on the Lord. If, however, you know what is the right thing to do, Paul says to do it. I describe it as a battle between the *will to* and the *want to*. You may not *want to* do right, you may not feel like doing right, but you must *will to* do right. We all make choices every day. Lots of people make the wrong choices because they do not care enough to do the right thing. Your *will to* do right must overcome your weak or sinful feelings. It is at this point Paul reinforces the promise of peace when he says, "…and the God of peace shall be with you." The peace that passes understanding in verse 7 may seem to be sent from a distance; but when we think right and do right, we are assured in verse 9 that our peace is brought to us by the very comforting presence of the Lord.

I will always remember a lady from my pastoral ministry. She was one of those young moms who was always upset about her children or school or something. I would have called her a nervous wreck. The time came when what seemed to be a long lingering chest cold was diagnosed as lung cancer. I visited her house and shared with her the message of Philippians 4.

I recall sitting in my study a few days later when I received a call. I answered the phone, and she simply said, "Pastor, I've got it."

"You have what?" I asked.

She replied, "Peace."

On December 26, 1986, Arlene's cancer became the pathway to her heavenly home. I saw the hand of God move in her heart and mind. The Lord did not change Arlene's circumstances, but He changed her with the peace that passes understanding. That same peace is offered to you and to me by the God of peace.

# CHAPTER SEVEN

# ESCAPING SELF-PITY AND BITTERNESS

*Hebrews 12:1–17*

¹ *Wherefore seeing we also are compassed about with so great a cloud of witnesses, let us lay aside every weight, and the sin which doth so easily beset us, and let us run with patience the race that is set before us,*

² *Looking unto Jesus the author and finisher of our faith; who for the joy that was set before him endured the cross, despising the shame, and is set down at the right hand of the throne of God.*

³ *For consider him that endured such contradiction of sinners against himself, lest ye be wearied and faint in your minds.*

⁴ *Ye have not yet resisted unto blood, striving against sin.*

⁵ *And ye have forgotten the exhortation which speaketh unto you as unto children, My son, despise not thou the chastening of the Lord, nor faint when thou art rebuked of him:*

⁶ *For whom the Lord loveth he chasteneth, and scourgeth every son whom he receiveth.*

⁷ *If ye endure chastening, God dealeth with you as with sons; for what son is he whom the father chasteneth not?*

⁸ *But if ye be without chastisement, whereof all are partakers, then are ye bastards, and not sons.*

⁹ *Furthermore we have had fathers of our flesh which corrected us, and*

*we gave them reverence: shall we not much rather be in subjection unto the Father of spirits, and live?*

*[10] For they verily for a few days chastened us after their own pleasure; but he for our profit, that we might be partakers of his holiness.*

*[11] Now no chastening for the present seemeth to be joyous, but grievous: nevertheless afterward it yieldeth the peaceable fruit of righteousness unto them which are exercised thereby.*

*[12] Wherefore lift up the hands which hang down, and the feeble knees:*

*[13] And make straight paths for your feet, lest that which is lame be turned out of the way; but let it rather be healed.*

*[14] Follow peace with all men, and holiness, without which no man shall see the Lord:*

*[15] Looking diligently lest any man fail of the grace of God; lest any root of bitterness springing up trouble you, and thereby many be defiled.*

*[16] Lest there be any fornicator, or profane person, as Esau, who for one morsel of meat sold his birthright.*

*[17] For ye know how that afterward, when he would have inherited the blessing, he was rejected: for he found no place of repentance, though he sought it carefully with tears.*

An understanding and acceptance of this text and its message provides wonderful help in getting victory over trials and heartaches. Some of the truths given here are found elsewhere in Scripture, but some are uniquely presented in this passage of the Bible.

Those who received this letter had suffered greatly, primarily for their faith in Christ. The response to trial required for them is the same response to trial that is required for us. To know some background of those who received this letter will help us understand the text. At some time in the past, these believers had suffered, but as it says in Hebrews 10: 34, they took it joyfully. Can you imagine that? That was amazing victory for them to experience as young believers. By the time they received this letter, however, they were not joyful. In fact, they had collapsed under the pressures and were struggling in spiritual defeat.

In Chapter 11 and leading into Chapter 12, they were introduced to the saints of old who went through much testing but experienced tremendous victory. The writer told the stories of Old Testament saints like Abel, Abraham, and Moses, as well as many unnamed believers who were tortured, mocked, and imprisoned. The purpose was to remind these new believers that others had suffered, just like they were suffering. Remember, one of Satan's methods of defeating us is to stir up feelings of self-pity, convincing us no one has suffered the way we have suffered. Beginning in the middle of Hebrews 12:1, the pathway to victory for these believers is laid out.

The goal given to these struggling Christians was to "run with patience the race that is set before us." The picture drawn with these words portrays our individual life as a race. Your life is the race God has set before you. It will have obstacles to hinder you and barriers to stop you, but you are to run it with patience. The term *patience* means endurance. When things get tough, too many people quit on the Lord and fail to fulfill their responsibilities. This is unacceptable. We need endurance.

For the sake of our own spiritual well-being, let's be aware that these Hebrew believers were not coddled in their tribulation by the writer. He certainly had compassion for them, but he let them know they had to take responsibility for their response to trials. The writer might be viewed as a bit harsh, but having people feel sorry for us never brings us the victory we need. Sympathy from others brings a measure of consolation, so the Lord tells us to bear one another's burdens; but true and lasting victory comes only from the Lord and His Word.

The writer's challenge in verse 1 is that we run our race of life with endurance, in spite of our troubles. In fact, he says we must lay aside the weights and sins that could hinder us. Have you noticed in your own life that when you are under a heavy burden you tend to lose your spiritual fervency? In other words, you sometimes do not care as much about doing right when you are under stress. I have talked to many people who justify sinful attitudes and spiritual failures in their lives by claiming that no one understands what they are going through. They say things like, "If you were going through what I am going through, you might do wrong things, too." The writer of Hebrews tells us just the opposite is necessary, reminding us that we must stay spiritually sharp during trial, rejecting sin and everything else that might hinder our spiritual walk. If you have developed something of an "I don't care" attitude, you must repent of it and draw close to the Lord.

In verses 2–4 the writer points us to the Lord Jesus Christ and the renewal of a spiritual and eternal perspective. The importance of this lesson cannot be overlooked. Time after time the writers of Scripture remind us, directly and indirectly, that this world is not our home and that the hurtful things which we go through must be seen in light of eternity and our relationship to the Lord. Verse 2 says, "Looking unto Jesus..." This phrase is carrying on the challenge of verse 1. We are to "run with patience (endurance)...looking unto Jesus." The word translated *looking* means to look away from one thing as if to see another. We must take our eyes off of our immediate trouble and look unto the Lord Jesus. How do we look unto Jesus and how does it help?

Verse 2 tells us about the Lord when He was on this earth. It says He "endured the cross." The word *endured* is the same term translated *patience* in verse 1. The text says He endured the cross "for (because of) the joy that was set before him" which was in essence the same joy that is set before us, namely heaven. The verse then confirms to us where the Lord Jesus is right now. He is seated at the right hand of the throne of God. As He is in heaven, someday you and I, who are saved, will also be in heaven. He has gone to prepare a place for us. If we can recognize how the reality and joy of heaven motivated our Savior to endure His earthly trials (especially the cross), we can endure our trial (cross), whatever it may be. The truth is, not one of us truly appreciates how wonderful heaven will be, and, therefore, fail in letting that truth motivate us to endure the relatively light burdens of our earthly walk.

Verse 3 tells us to consider or weigh carefully what Christ went through so we will not "be wearied and faint" in our minds. To be weary and faint means to get tired and quit. The word translated *mind* is actually the word that is most often translated soul. The soul includes not only the mind, but also the will, emotions, and conscience. The writer knew the danger of people getting so overcome by their troubles that they would quit mentally and emotionally and make very bad choices in life. In verse 4 he takes the challenge one step further by calling on them to compare their sufferings with those of the Lord Jesus. He reminded them that they had not yet resisted unto blood, striving against sin. The Lord Jesus went to the cross because of the sin of the world. He gave all in death, yet He was without sin. He never did one thing wrong, yet He suffered so greatly. Can our suffering be compared to His? Ask the Lord to deepen your anticipation of the joy of heaven. It will be worth it all when we enter heaven and stand before the Lord. What will be worth it all? Not just suffering—being victorious in suffering.

In the next seven verses we are taught, as we have seen in other texts, that there is divine purpose in everything. To seek and accept that purpose will put us on a pathway to victory. We will not consider these verses in depth, but there are truths we must not pass by. In verse 5 the writer almost chides the people by telling them that part of their defeat was due to the fact that they had forgotten an exhortation from the book of Proverbs. He then quotes from Proverbs 3:11 which says that we must not despise the chastening of the Lord nor faint when rebuked of Him. It is implied that these believers were in fact despising what God was doing in their lives. The particular word translated *despise* means to take lightly or disregard. What they were disregarding was the chastening of the Lord.

Chastening is training and instruction. Too often, when things go wrong in our lives, we totally disregard the training purposes which the Lord has in mind when He allows or brings on the difficulty. When we miss the Lord's purpose, it is easy to *faint* in the midst of the trouble. To faint means to give in or give up. If you are at that point, ready to give in or give up, cry out to the Lord and ask Him to help you grasp His purpose in your trial.

The next few verses teach us that chastening in our lives is an evidence of God's love toward us and proof that we are children of God. The message is simple. If parents love their children, they train them, and parents only train their own. Our loving heavenly Father loves us as His children, so He trains us. The trials of life are part of God's training program for us. Do you realize that the trouble and heartache you are facing right now has been allowed by God to train and instruct you as one of His children?

In time of trial many people question God's love. The Bible says that trial is the evidence of God's love. If you are a parent, you know that the training and discipline of your children is an essential part of parenting. Your child does not always like it, nor does he respond well to it, but it is necessary for his proper development. The parent who fails to train his child could properly be accused of neglect. The Lord sees the necessity of our training, and He is faithful to His task as our Heavenly Father.

Consider the teaching of verses 10 and 11 to see how the Lord uses trial and trouble to deepen our faith and cause us to grow spiritually. In verse 10 the writer compares earthly fathers with God, our Heavenly Father. He says that earthly fathers chasten their children "after their own pleasure." Earthly fathers do not always act in the best interest of their children, and even if that is their desire, they do not always know what is best. When you are born again, you become a true child of God. From that point on you can rest in this—the Lord, your Heavenly Father, will always know what is best for you and will always do what is best for you. You need to believe that right now. You may not feel that what has happened could possibly be the best for you, but claim that truth by faith. The middle of verse 10 expresses it this way—"But he for our profit." Whatever the Lord allows in your life is for your profit. *Profit* means to be for your advantage or to make you better. Will you spiritually profit from your current situation? That is God's plan and desire. Will you be defeated or destroyed? That is exactly what Satan desires.

Verse 10 goes on and says, "that we might be partakers of his holiness." Profiting from trial includes partaking of the Lord's holiness. In other words, He wants our trouble in life to make us more like Christ and to develop in us an abhorrence for sin. We should hate sin. Its presence in this world is the source of all heartache. Unfortunately, the presence of sin not only underlies the tribulations that come into our lives, but sometimes controls our responses to those tribulations. In other words, rather than responding in a spiritual way in the face of trial, we sometimes say wrong things, do wrong things, think wrong things, or develop wrong attitudes. Trying experiences, which could bring profit to our lives, become wasted experiences. We suffer in vain. We must always ask the Lord to make our trials profitable. We do not want to go through hard times and then have those experiences wasted through a hardened heart or sinful responses on our part.

Life is not easy. Our Lord wants us to know He understands how hard life can be. He says in verse 11, "Now no chastening...seemeth to be joyous, but grievous." Do you know the Lord understands exactly how you feel? Remember Hebrews 4:15 which tells us our Lord Jesus Christ is "touched with the feelings of our infirmities" because He "was in all points tempted like as we are." The word *touched* means to have compassion. Our Lord has compassion toward us in our hard times. He understands that chastening is grievous. Most often people do not really understand what we are going through. They may want to, but they cannot. The Lord does. He can relieve our heartaches, even using them to produce spiritual good in our lives.

Think about the rest of verse 11, "...nevertheless afterward it (the chastening experience) yieldeth the peaceable (peaceful) fruit of righteousness unto them which are exercised thereby." **Afterward,** yes, praise the Lord, *there is always an afterward.* Sometimes in crisis we feel there will never be a way out. It is like we are peering into a deep dark hole without hope. The Lord wants us to look beyond the crisis to a time of comfort and restoration.

Look what the Lord wants to bring out of your difficult experience. The word *yieldeth* does not simply mean to produce; it means to give back or reward. What a picture is given here of chastening! Every time we go through chastening, the experience gives back, repays, and rewards us with spiritual fruit in our lives. At this moment you may not be able to see any value in spiritual fruit. You may simply wish the trouble had never come, but do not quit on the Lord. You need that spiritual fruit when you are in physical, emotional, or mental turmoil. It is called the peaceable or peaceful fruit of righteousness. Even in grievous (sorrowful) trial, the Lord wants to give us that peace that passes understanding (Philippians 4:7).

> *Afterward...*
> *there is always*
> *an afterward.*

You may desperately need that peace now. Being filled with that peace diminishes anger, hurt, and frustration. It is then that the Lord can bring us to new levels of righteousness. When we are struggling, it is absolutely essential that we do right. Doing the wrong thing in pressured times magnifies and multiplies our problems. Believe me, you need this spiritual fruit. Ask the Lord to produce it in you beginning now.

The writer of Hebrews puts one condition on this pathway to growth in righteousness. He said it is for "them which are exercised thereby." The term *exercise* speaks of training in the gym and is used here to suggest the training of mind and heart that comes through life's trials. You and I have choices to make in times of difficulty. Now may be a time for you to make a choice. The test you are going through may totally defeat you and leave you worse off spiritually and emotionally than before the trial came. Or you can cast yourself on God's mercy and grace asking Him to help you learn, grow, and be spiritually strengthened through the trial. Your response will make the difference. The Hebrews were making wrong choices. Verses 12 and 13 tell us what was happening.

In verse 12 the writer challenges them to "lift up the hands which hang down, and the feeble knees." Hands hanging down is a picture of self-pity. Woe is me! Listen, you and I cannot live with self-pity. Then hands hanging down portrays weakness and exhaustion. We feel sorry for ourselves and cannot understand why these things happen to us.

Feeble knees portrays paralysis, as by a stroke. We cannot go on; we cannot take any more. The Lord is striking a perfect balance in this text between compassion for hurting people (verses 10–11) and exhortation to responsible living, in spite of hurt (verses 12–13). He tells us He understands exactly how we feel and He cares for us, but our hurts cannot be allowed to paralyze us emotionally and spiritually. We must go on!

Verse 13 tells us to "make straight paths for our feet." Get up, get going again, renew purpose in your life. Look to the Lord for direction. He gives a warning when He says, "Lest that which is lame be turned out of the way." To be *lame* is to be crippled, which is bad, but to be *turned out of the way* means to be totally out of joint, which is worse. He is telling us that if we refuse to do right, things will only get worse.

He concludes the verse by saying, "But let it rather be healed." The meaning of healing is obvious, but it is elsewhere translated "be made whole." That thought may help us here because we often feel we can never be whole again in light of the trial with which we have been afflicted. It is true that *things* may never be the same, but you can be whole again. You can have peace, strength, courage, and joy if you will let the Lord give it to you. I know you may not want to go on. You just want to be left alone to sulk and console yourself. You feel life has been unfair. You have tried your best and for what? But you must seek the Lord for the next step in your life. Let the Lord bring healing into your life.

The next few verses encourage us to stay spiritually focused. When we are going through hard times, we are vulnerable to spiritual defeat. We must not let our trials take us off our spiritual course. It happens all the time in the lives of Christians. Do not let it happen to you!

Verse 14 gives us two exhortations and one warning. The exhortations are "Follow peace with all men, and holiness…" Many times our problems are related to people. What others say and do can hurt us deeply. The writer instructs us to follow or pursue peace with people. You and I must not hold a grudge against any person—first of all, because our battle is not with people. Remember Ephesians 6:12, "For we wrestle not against flesh and blood, but against principalities, against powers, against the rulers of the darkness of this world, against spiritual wickedness in high places." You may feel like certain people are your enemies. They may be, but they cannot ultimately bring harm to you. You are in the Lord's hands. Let them say what they want to say and do what they want to do. They may not be following biblical teaching, but you must. Trust the

Lord to take care of you. Treat others right, regardless of how they treat you. A second reason you must not hold a grudge is because there is a great day coming when hearts will be manifest and all things will be made right. Wait patiently for that day.

The second instruction in the verse is "follow...holiness." Make the basic goal of your life to become like Christ. In every trial ask your Heavenly Father to make you more like the Lord Jesus. We must obey these exhortations for many reasons, but especially because of the warning that comes after them. The warning is "without which no man shall see the Lord." The key word here is *see*. It means to perceive and discern. It is important to discern what the Lord is doing as He allows our trials. When things go wrong we need to seek the Lord, asking Him to show us what He is doing and what we are to learn. If, however, we get emotionally and spiritually defeated by holding a grudge against someone or if we set aside our goal of becoming like Christ, we will never find the Lord in the midst of our heartache. If we do not stay in close communion with Him, we may be prone to fall into deep sin.

As I grew up, my family was a disaster. Ours was a broken home which translated into low income, lonely hours, no dad, running the streets, and wrong friends. Victory came when I got saved and could begin to grasp why the Lord allowed me to grow up that way. He used it to develop strong marriage and parenting convictions that have brought immeasurable blessing to my adult life. As we saw in an earlier text, I realized that the years of my youth was not a matter of what happened *to me*, but what happened *for me*.

Verses 15–17 continue the warning of what can happen in our lives if we do not learn the lessons and get the victory and healing God has for us. It is not only the tragedy of missing God's purpose for our trials, but also the possibility of plunging into life-destroying sin. There are three dangers of which we must beware. Our spiritual and emotional defeat makes us very vulnerable to them all. The first is bitterness. Verse 15 tells us to look diligently for God's purpose in our trials. If we do not, we may "fail of the grace of God." We have seen in other texts that during our troubles God's grace is available and will be sufficient to get us through. Remember that II Corinthians 4:15 teaches us that giving thanks opens the door to God's abundant grace. What if we "fail of the grace of God?" If we refuse to let the Lord minister to us by His grace, we are on our own and we will end up bitter. Bitterness is a poison that ruins our lives and the lives of those around us. It is described as a root. It goes deeply into our being producing trouble for us and defilement in everyone around us. We must not become bitter.

The second danger is mentioned in verse 16, "Lest there be any fornicator." When we are discouraged, we are most vulnerable to immorality. Some people plan their sin. Many are ensnared at a weak moment. Neither is acceptable to God. I think of a couple who lost a child in death. They were defeated and failed to minister to each other. In discouragement one turned to someone else for comfort. The immoral situation that developed destroyed the marriage. Their other two children grew up in a broken home, each eventually married, but both ended up divorced. Did it all have to turn out that way? I will never believe it had to.

The third danger is also found in verse 16 where we read, "…or profane person." To be profane means to cross a line, usually to violate what God calls holy with no ability to cross back at a later time. The writer gives us an illustration of a profane person by reminding us of Esau. Esau had little regard for spiritual things, so for a bit of pottage (Genesis 25:30–34) he sold his birthright. As the oldest son in his family the birthright would have made him head of the family physically and spiritually at his father's death. He did not care. Hebrews 12:17 says, "For ye know how that afterward, when he would have inherited the blessing, he was rejected." Take notice of the term *afterward* and remember **there is always an afterward.** Yes, the time came when Esau's father was about to die and Esau would have inherited his blessing, but it was too late. In a moment of greed, foolishness, and mere worldly thinking, he gave up his future blessings. Short-sightedness destroyed what might have been. How many times I have heard the warning to not make long term decisions while under emotional or spiritual stress. How many times I have witnessed people doing that very thing. Often they come back later bemoaning what they had done, but by that time it was too late. They cry out wishing they had done differently, but there was no way back.

Bitterness, fornication, and profane living mark the lives of many who miss God's purpose and find no victory in the midst of trial. The gracious offer of the Lord must be restated here. "But let it rather be healed." The story of Joseph stands out as a wonderful testimony of one who had every earthly reason to give in to sin and self-pity, but stayed faithful to the Lord. At age 17 he was sold into slavery by his brothers. He could have ended up in bitterness, but he did not. At age 28 he was pursued by Potiphar's wife, who tried to draw him into immorality. He might have felt justified in sin, feeling that God had failed him by letting him become a slave. Why should he be loyal to God? But he was loyal to God and rejected the fornication. He could have totally lived for himself and rejected his brethren when they came searching for food twenty years after selling him as a slave. By this time, however, Joseph had been healed. He saw God's purpose in his slavery and found wonderful victory. Joseph could tell his brothers, who had been his greatest enemies, "Now therefore be not grieved, nor angry with yourselves, that ye sold me hither: for God did send me before you to preserve life...So now it was not you that sent me hither, but God." (Genesis 45:5, 8) Later in Genesis 50:20, he said, "But as for you, ye thought evil against me; but God meant it unto good."

One of the most meaningful lessons in my life came when a plan for ministry that had moved us 800 miles and cost us almost all we had fell apart. There were people we could have blamed, who perhaps intended some things for evil, but our victory came from looking for God's purpose. It was so much sweeter to believe that "God meant it unto good." That is where you will find your victory.

# CHAPTER EIGHT

# HUMILITY AS A PATHWAY TO GRACE

*I Peter 5:5b–11*

*5b Yea, all of you be subject one to another, and be clothed with humility: for God resisteth the proud, and giveth grace to the humble.*

*6 Humble yourselves therefore under the mighty hand of God, that he may exalt you in due time:*

*7 Casting all your care upon him; for he careth for you.*

*8 Be sober, be vigilant; because your adversary the devil, as a roaring lion, walketh about, seeking whom he may devour:*

*9 Whom resist stedfast in the faith, knowing that the same afflictions are accomplished in your brethren that are in the world.*

*10 But the God of all grace, who hath called us unto his eternal glory by Christ Jesus, after that ye have suffered a while, make you perfect, stablish, strengthen, settle you.*

*11 To him be glory and dominion for ever and ever. Amen.*

In facing trials no text has been more personally meaningful to me than this one. That is because it is the one to which the Lord brought me in what, to this point in my life, has been my greatest time of trial. In itself it stands as one text among many which the Lord has given to help us understand trials and how to get victory over them. For me it opened a pathway to personal victory that I had not found in any other passage.

Much of the first epistle of Peter was written regarding trial and suffering. Encouragement was given in I Peter 1:6–9 for these believers who were "in heaviness through manifold temptations." In Chapter 2:18–23 servants were given special exhortation to take suffering patiently and follow the example of the Savior, who "when he was reviled, reviled not again." In I Peter 3:14 the saints were consoled with these words, "But and if ye suffer for righteousness' sake, happy are ye." In I Peter 4:12 the reminder came to "think it not strange concerning the fiery trial which is to try you, as though some strange thing happened unto you."

As Peter concludes his letter, he gives the passage from chapter 5 quoted in the beginning of this chapter. These 6½ verses are filled with meaningful instructions to lead us to the victory we need when things are going wrong all around us. We start with the middle of verse 5 because Peter has completed one thought in the first part of the verse. The second part of the verse lays the foundation for his discussion on getting victory in the midst of trial.

He begins by cautioning the struggling believers to be subject one to another and, in fact, to be clothed with humility. Being proud and self-centered brings division, especially in hard times when nerves are on edge. These suffering saints needed unity to be victorious over their circumstances. Peter introduced this idea earlier in the epistle with exhortations like "Finally, be ye all of one mind, having compassion one of another, love as brethren, be pitiful, be courteous" (3:8). He further said, "And above all things have fervent charity (love) among yourselves: for charity shall cover the multitude of sins" (4:8). He knew that in the midst of trial the believers could easily get frustrated and turn against each other. It was important that they stay very close to each other, to bear up under the pressures coming against them. Pressure on a marriage, family, or in a church will either drive people together or drive people apart.

In the midst of trouble there must not be contention, and as Proverbs 13:10 says, "Only by pride cometh contention." During troublesome times we need to take the low road; we need to be sensitive to those around us who are also struggling. Our whole demeanor needs to be marked by humbleness or as the verse puts it—we must be "clothed with humility." If you are facing hard times right now, it may be that the pressures of the situation have caused division between you and the people who are closest to you. Just when you need each other the most, you are quarreling. Stop! You must humbly turn to each other and tenderly draw near to each other. You need each other. You may feel quite justified in having said some things that have hurt others during this time of trial. You may feel they have been insensitive or hardhearted, but you must not let the seeming callousness in another produce a similar response in you. You cannot control the other person, but you must do the right thing. As we will see in the next paragraph, there is even more at stake than your fellowship with and consolation from those around you.

Humility will not only keep us close to other people in trying times, but it will also open the door for the Lord's help. Peter says, "For God resisteth the proud, and giveth grace to the humble." Pride is a destroyer. It is the sin that took Lucifer down, and it can take us down. Proverbs 6:16–17 tells us that the Lord hates pride and that the proud look is an abomination to Him. We realize that pride is a serious sin when the Bible says that God resists the proud. To *resist* means to oppose. When things go wrong, we tend to react in pride against people and sometimes against the Lord Himself. We can become angry, bitter, and vengeful. It is our pride that causes us to react with deep hurt at what people did or what the Lord allowed. Then we look for the Lord to step in and change things. At that point, however, the Lord may be far from helping us because our pride is causing Him to oppose us. He only gives grace to the humble. To be *humble* does not mean that we refuse to stand up for right or that we allow wrong to go unchecked. It does mean that we guard our attitude and approach to the people who have hurt us. We reject headiness and high-mindedness in dealing with problems.

As to our direct response to the Lord, Peter makes the challenge very clear in verse 6. He says, "Humble yourselves therefore under the mighty hand of God." To *humble ourselves* before the Lord means that we bend, bow, and submit to Him. It is to recognize His divine purpose in our lives, as we have seen in other texts. Humbling ourselves before the Lord demonstrates that same spirit seen in the Lord Jesus— "…not my will but thine be done" (Luke 22:42). It acknowledges our total dependence on the Lord to get victory. Peter tells us that to humble ourselves is necessary so "he (God) may exalt you in due time."

Sometimes trouble turns people away from the Lord. I have seen it too often. Even now you may not be as close to Him as you should be. Rather than running to Him, you may have pulled away. But where will you turn if you do not turn to Him? Where will you find comfort and peace, if not from Him? You need to humble yourself before Him immediately. Express your humility before the Lord in prayer. Tell Him you submit

to Him. Tell Him you are willing for His will to be done. Tell Him you
acknowledge His right to do or allow in your life anything He deems
best. Peter says the Lord will not let us stay down if we humble ourselves
before Him, but He will exalt us in due time. He will lift us up in just the
right way, at just the right time. He may change the circumstances we are
facing or He may give us the necessary strength to go on, but either way,
He will be there for us.

If we hang on to pride, however, we do not get God's help. Verse 7 carries
on the thought of humbling ourselves before the Lord when it says,
"Casting all your care upon him; for he careth for you." In other words,
part of humbling ourselves before the Lord is the action of casting or
throwing all our care on Him. To cast our care upon Him acknowledges
our need for His grace. "Lord, I cannot make it without You. I cannot
handle it without You. I cannot go on without You." We are told to cast
our care on Him "for he careth for you." That means He takes care of
us. Give God your cares because He is the One who takes care of you. He
has always taken care of you. Are we foolish enough to think that all this
time we have been taking care of ourselves?

In verses 8–9 Peter alerts us to the fact that every problem we have is
ultimately a spiritual matter. We must not miss that truth. Why? Because
the Devil is looking for people whom he may devour and the easiest to
devour are those who are in a weakened state. His exhortation begins,
"Be sober, be vigilant…" To *be sober* means to be steady, to not fear, panic,
or get angry. When things go wrong, we often respond emotionally. We
can panic or be overcome with fear very easily. Sometimes our reaction is
more characterized by anger and a desire to get back at someone. Being
controlled by any of these emotions leaves us vulnerable to saying and
doing the wrong things. The Lord wants us to be steady and stable, to
think clearly, and to respond spiritually.

Peter says, "Be vigilant." We need to be alert to what is happening, and
we need to be aware of Satan's tactics. Peter spoke from experience. In
the Garden of Gethsemane, Peter should have been prayerfully vigilant,
but he fell asleep. In the most critical time of God's plan for redemption,
Peter was unaware of the spiritual conflict going on around him. The
Lord Jesus found him sleeping. His words to Peter are recorded in Mark
14:37–38, "Sleepest thou? Couldest not thou watch one hour? Watch
ye and pray, lest ye enter into temptation. The spirit truly is ready, but
the flesh is weak." Peter went back to sleep, and by the time he woke
up, it was too late. In the confusion of the Savior's arrest, he reacted by

taking his sword and cutting off the ear of Malchus, who was a servant of the High Priest. The Lord Jesus healed the ear and rebuked Peter. If Peter had been watching and praying, he might have done the right thing. If he had been steady and vigilant, he might have stood with Christ and accompanied Him to His trial. Instead, he used the sword against Malchus, and then he fled with others forsaking the Lord. Then he followed along behind the crowd who took Christ and, finally, when confronted, denied that he even knew Him. What a victory for the Devil. Yes, Peter knew what he was talking about when he warned us of the Adversary and told us we must be sober and vigilant. Weariness and emotional stress can dull our spiritual senses and open the door to great defeat, but we must not let that happen.

The rest of the warning in verse 8 is stated this way, "...because your adversary the devil, as a roaring lion, walketh about, seeking whom he may devour." You must recognize, as we said earlier, that the problem you face today is ultimately spiritual. To you it may seem to be people or finances or disease, but God lets us know it is spiritual. You have a spiritual adversary. You have someone who hates you and wants to destroy you. He will make use of financial difficulty or an unkind person to undermine your walk with God. He will kill your joy and take your peace. This enemy is the Devil. He is not just fighting the Lord, he is seeking people like you and me so he can devour us. To put it in simple terms, he wants to ruin your life. He has been extremely successful in the lives of others. Will he succeed with you? If you refuse the teaching of the Word of God, he will have his way.

In verse 9 Peter tells us to resist the Devil, and he tells us how. Before we discuss that, it is helpful to remember James 4:7 which says, "Submit yourselves therefore to God." That is what Peter teaches us in verses 6–7. Then James goes on and says, "Resist the devil, and he will flee from you." Thank you, James, for informing us that if we resist the Devil he will flee. This adversary who hates us will go away, at least for awhile. We need to know how to resist him. We return to Peter for that counsel. He says, "Whom (the devil) resist stedfast in the faith, knowing that the same afflictions are accomplished in your brethren that are in the world." We resist the Devil steadfast in the faith. What does that mean? Find the promises of God in the Bible. Believe them. Claim them. Do not let them go. When our Lord Jesus came under Satanic attack as recorded in Matthew 4 and Luke 4, He responded with the Scriptures. That is exactly what you and I must do. Recorded on the next page are some of God's promises for born-again Christians. If you are saved, they are for you.

> *For this God is our God for ever and ever: he will be our guide even unto death. (Psalm 48:14)*

> *The Lord is nigh unto all them that call upon him, to all that call upon him in truth. (Psalm 145:18)*

> *Trust in the Lord with all thine heart; and lean not unto thine own understanding. In all thy ways acknowledge him, and he shall direct thy paths. (Proverbs 3:5–6)*

> *There hath no temptation taken you but such as is common to man: but God is faithful, who will not suffer (allow) you to be tempted above that ye are able; but will with the temptation also make a way to escape, that ye may be able to bear it. (I Corinthians 10:13)*

> *For he hath said, I will never leave thee, nor forsake thee. (Hebrews 13:5b)*

> *If we confess our sins, he is faithful and just to forgive us our sins, and to cleanse us from all unrighteousness. (I John 1:9)*

You can find hundreds more of God's promises to you. Believe them, claim them, and do not let them go. Your steadfastness in claiming these promises will drive the Devil away. You cannot resist the Devil successfully in any other way. Remember again, the Scriptures are what the Lord Jesus used when He was tempted. The Scriptures are what you and I must also use.

As we come to verses 10–11 in I Peter 5 we are told that our problems are spiritual, not only because of Satan's involvement, but also because the Lord is involved, too. If we have trouble and try to handle it without the help of the Lord, we will be in greater trouble. Verse 10 begins with "But the God of all grace…" When we humble ourselves, pride is conquered, and we open the door to the abundant grace of God. Without God's grace the blessings introduced in this verse are not available to us. Through God's grace we can experience them.

The next phrase in verse 10 is "who hath called us unto his eternal glory by Christ Jesus…" Before telling us of God's gracious blessings, Peter wants us to renew our eternal perspective. He reminds us of our heavenly calling in Christ. How often we have seen, in this brief examination of Scripture passages, that a deep appreciation of our heavenly home will go a long way in carrying us through earthly trials. The certainty of heaven and the enabling grace of God will bring us sweet victory in the midst of our hard times.

After reminding us of our heavenly calling, Peter says, "After that ye have suffered a while…" Here is another truth we have seen elsewhere in our study—**there is always an afterward.** Peter says that after we have suffered a while God will do certain things. We must notice these promises do not include a guarantee of change in circumstances, rather they offer a change in us. I am sure you are like me—you want the circumstances to change. Sometimes they do, sometimes they don't.

What is God promising to do? The verse says He will "make you perfect, stablish, strengthen, and settle you." He will, first of all, use our troublesome experiences to make us *perfect*. The word *perfect*, as you may know, does not refer to sinless perfection. It does refer to a growing and maturing process. When we are born again, we are spiritual infants. We get fed through the Scriptures to grow in knowledge. We go through trials to grow in spiritual grace. It is parallel to our physical experience. When we are born, we are physical infants. We are fed with physical food. If we only took in food and never exercised, we would be fat and unable to move. We would have no strength. We would be unable to walk, run, and function normally. Babies must learn to walk. Learning to walk involves many trying experiences, including falling and perhaps getting hurt. Every one of us who is able to walk, however, is grateful that we had those falls and hurts which produced the physical development we needed.

> *Victory does not always include a change in circumstances, but it will always include a change in you.*

For us to grow and function properly in our spiritual lives, we will have to fall and get hurt from time to time. We must remember that this spiritual maturing process is accomplished by the grace of God. If we refuse to humble ourselves before the Lord, we will not receive that grace, nor will we grow one spiritual inch through our trials. The Lord wants to make your troublesome time a growing experience for you. There is nothing wrong with asking Him to change your circumstances, but make sure to also ask Him to help you grow spiritually through this time of trial.

The second thing the Lord will do is to *stablish* us. To *stablish* or *establish* means to make something fixed, as in concrete. It is to make something stable and no longer shaky. Trials and troubles can shake us. Our faith can weaken, and our trust in the Lord can diminish. When we open ourselves to God's grace, just the opposite happens. We see Satan for who he is and what he is trying to do. And we see the Lord for who He is and what He is trying to do. Then our faith is fixed. We will be better prepared if and when the next trial comes. Ask the Lord to use this trying time to make you more stable spiritually and emotionally than you have ever been before.

Then Peter says the Lord will *strengthen* us. As we noted in the previous paragraph, trials can weaken us. When we experience the grace of God, they strengthen us. We become stronger in heart, mind, will, and determination. Pray for the Lord to strengthen you. None of us want more trials, but we want to be ready to handle anything this world brings our way.

Finally, Peter says the Lord will *settle* us. Christians today seem quite shallow in their commitment to Christ and their dedication to His cause. To *settle* speaks of a deepening process. God in His grace will deepen our faith through trials. We will get more serious about the things that really matter. We will have a deeper appreciation of spiritual truths. The church as a body is spiritually shallow, especially in our country. When we meet those from others lands who have gone through much suffering for Christ, there is a depth about their life and their faith, of which we know little. As we, one by one, experience trials in our lives, God in His grace will greatly deepen our relationship with Him. Often in tribulation people feel like the Lord has forgotten them or deserted them. Instead the Lord is ready to give us greater victories than we might imagine possible. No wonder Peter says in verse 11, "To him be glory and dominion for ever and ever. Amen."

## CHAPTER NINE

# FOCUSING ON THE REAL ENEMY

*Ephesians 6:12*

*12 For we wrestle not against flesh and blood, but against principalities, against powers, against the rulers of the darkness of this world, against spiritual wickedness in high places.*

The entire passage of Ephesians 6:10–20 is worthy of our study, but for the purpose of this discussion we will focus our attention on verse 12. If you are going through trial right now, you are wrestling. The question to be answered is "Against what or whom are you wrestling?" Great defeat can come when people have been involved in creating or enlarging our troubles. The Apostle Paul wants us to understand, however, that people are not the ultimate enemy. Think of what people did to him. People failed him, lied about him, forsook him, stoned him, imprisoned him, and beat him. He recognized, however, his battle was with Satan and his emissaries.

The same is true for you and me. During my life I have had people seek to undermine my ministry by lying and spreading false rumors. What have people done to you? I am sure there could be quite a list, but if we focus on people we will fall into great defeat. We serve the Lord, not people. He is the One who opens doors, and no one closes them. He is the One who closes doors, and no one opens them. In other words, people cannot harm us. We are in the Lord's hands. Nothing can happen to us unless the Lord allows it. Take your eyes off people. Your real enemy is Satan. He can destroy you by stealing your joy and peace or taking away your zeal for serving Christ. If Paul could see past the people, so can we. Do we wrestle? Yes, but not against flesh and blood.

In II Corinthians 2:10–11 Paul writes, "To whom ye forgive any thing, I forgive also: for if I forgave any thing, to whom I forgave it, for your sakes forgave I it in the person of Christ; Lest Satan should get an advantage of us: for we are not ignorant of his devices." The circumstances surrounding this statement involved terrible sin in the church. Paul had addressed it in his first letter, and, apparently, the guilty party had confessed his sin. Now, the issue became forgiveness. Paul recognized this was more than a mere matter among men. This was a spiritual matter, and Satan was involved. Would the Devil be able to use human conflict for success in his spiritual warfare? Paul knew he could and he would.

The Apostle was not ignorant of Satan's devices. The term *devices* means strategies. Satan has his ways of dealing with men, and they have been extremely successful since the beginning of time. If we refuse to forgive another person, Satan gets an advantage over us. Human sin is serious, and if someone sins against us, there is a biblically prescribed way of dealing with it. It does not end with the other person however. The real enemy stands ready to take full advantage of us and bring us lasting spiritual defeat. Paul saw the situation clearly and knew the spiritual implications involved in responding to this important matter. Forgiveness toward the offending brother would help the other brother, but it would also defeat the real enemy, Satan.

> *Nothing can happen to us unless the Lord allows it.*

In II Corinthians 12 the Apostle Paul gives testimony of wonderful revelation that the Lord had made known to him. In verse 7 of that chapter, Paul wrote, "And lest I should be exalted above measure through the abundance of the revelations, there was given to me a thorn in the flesh, the messenger of Satan to buffet me, lest I should be exalted above measure."

Many believe Paul's thorn in the flesh was a physical ailment that affected his eyesight. As you may know, he asked the Lord three times to take the problem away, but the Lord did not heal the physical disease. The Lord's response was the promise of sufficient grace to sustain Paul for continued service and joy in Christ. Paul had a clear understanding that the Lord allowed the problem to keep him humble. The Lord could have healed it, but He did not. At the same time, Paul clearly saw that Satan was the ultimate source of the attack. His physical problem could not ruin his life. Satan could. The thorn in the flesh was the messenger of Satan. This was spiritual warfare. In himself Paul could not bring about victory, but the Lord's grace in Paul's life kept Satan from defeating Paul.

So many Christians have physical problems. They range from daily aches and pains to heart problems or cancer. These problems are a thorn in the flesh. They hurt and are not easy to endure. Could the Lord heal them? Yes. Whether He does or not, however, will not determine our spiritual condition. God's grace will be sufficient for us to maintain joy and peace unless the real enemy, Satan, succeeds in bringing us down spiritually and emotionally.

In Acts 5 the newly formed church was shaken by the sin of Ananias and Sapphira and, all the more, by the swift judgment of God in taking their lives. Verse 11 says, "And great fear came upon all the church, and upon as many as heard these things." There is no doubt that Ananias and Sapphira were held accountable for their sin. It cost them their lives. At the same time, there was no hesitation on the part of Peter when he confronted them to say, "Why hath Satan filled thine heart to lie to the Holy Ghost?" (5:3) Ananias and Sapphira sinned before people, but their sin began when they yielded to the temptation of Satan.

As we have already seen in our study of I Peter 5, it is the Devil who goes about as a roaring lion seeking whom he may devour and we must resist him. In James 4:7 we read, "Submit yourselves therefore to God. Resist the devil, and he will flee from you." This truth, that Satan is the real enemy, needs to be understood and emphasized. On the one hand, too many of us get focused on other people. That is the pathway to sure defeat. What people say and do can be unpleasant for us, to say the least. It is Satan, however, who can destroy us. Refuse to let him have his way.

Another reason we must emphasize the fact that Satan is the real enemy is because many have developed a twisted view of the Lord and His dealings with men. Our God is sovereign to be sure, but that truth does not mean that God directly controls every detailed event of our lives. Does God allow things to happen? Yes. Does that mean He is to be held accountable for every thing that happens? No. I hear many people say, "Why did God do that?" I would ask, "Why do you blame God for it?" In all that the Apostle Paul went through, he never held the Lord accountable as the source of his trouble. To Paul, the Lord was always his source of strength and comfort. There is a growing view of the sovereignty of God, in some circles, that is out of harmony with scriptural teaching. That

God is sovereign means He has absolute authority—it does not mean that He directly controls every minute detail of life.

As Christians we are strangers and pilgrims on the earth. Satan is the prince of this world and the god of this age. The Lord Jesus judged Satan on the cross, but He has yet to come back and reclaim this world for Himself. In this worldly system we are the outsiders—we are here as ambassadors for Christ, serving Him until we are called home to heaven. We are Satan's enemy, and we are on his territory. We should not be surprised when he seeks to attack us, using people or circumstances.

When the attack comes, we run to the Lord for help. This is what gives meaning to Romans 8:28. "And we know that all things work together for good to them that love God, to them who are the called according to his purpose." The sovereign God does not create our problems. He, in His sovereignty, can take them and work them for good. I Corinthians 10:13 says, "There hath no temptation taken you but such as is common to man: but God is faithful, who will not suffer (allow) you to be tempted above that ye are able; but will with the temptation, also make a way to escape, that ye may be able to bear it." This verse does not show the Lord to be the source of the trouble. He, in His sovereignty, allows (suffers) us to be tempted, but controls the situation so the problem will not be more than we can bear. He is the source of our help.

The way some people look at life there is no place for a devil. That is why many people are carrying bitterness toward God. Instead of seeing Him as their source of help and comfort, they are blaming Him for the things that have gone wrong. This perverted view may have been spurred along by an effort to stop people from excusing their own guilt, by having a "the devil made me do it" attitude. We must see Satan as the enemy, but we are responsible for our actions. Our victory can only come when we have a right view of God, the Devil, and ourselves. Satan is the enemy. The Lord is our only source of help. We can have victory over Satan by trusting and obeying the Lord.

We must see our struggles as spiritual warfare. When we do, we can find victory.

# CHAPTER TEN

# PATHWAY TO FREEDOM

*Ephesians 4:30–32*

<sup>30</sup> *And grieve not the holy Spirit of God, whereby ye are sealed unto the day of redemption.*

<sup>31</sup> *Let all bitterness, and wrath, and anger, and clamour, and evil speaking, be put away from you, with all malice.*

<sup>32</sup> *And be ye kind one to another, tenderhearted, forgiving one another, even as God for Christ's sake hath forgiven you.*

These few verses have a strong message for each of us who have been hurt by other people. The lesson God wants us to learn is essential to our victory. Not only can we suffer from the hurt, but we can also lose the opportunity to be used by God for His service and glory. Does that matter? In the depths of despair we may not care whether or not we are usable, but when we get thinking straight again, we will realize how critical it is to our spiritual well-being.

The Apostle Paul begins with the warning to "grieve not the holy Spirit of God." The way this is written suggests that the believers in Ephesus were already grieving Him. We might render the early part of this verse this way: *Stop grieving the Holy Spirit of God.* He graciously reminds them that it was by the Holy Spirit that they were sealed unto the day of redemption. This is a marvelous truth for Christians. When we were saved, we were sealed. We were marked (sealed) by the Spirit of God as being His possession. There is no chance of losing God's wonderful salvation because the seal will continue until the day of our redemption. The day of our redemption is the day we go to heaven.

Being sealed and kept by the power of God is wonderful, but Paul says we must not grieve the Spirit. The way we grieve the Holy Spirit is by sinning as described in verse 31. He tells us we must get rid of the bitterness, wrath, anger, clamor, evil speaking, and malice that we carry in our hearts and perhaps express in unkind ways to others. It has been suggested that grieving the Spirit creates a situation where the Lord has to work on us instead of working through us. The Lord wants to use us for His glory, but when we grieve the Spirit we are unfit to be used.

How do we end up living in verse 31? I dare say no one plans to become bitter or angry as they start a day. We may go out with great hope for a good day, but as the day goes on someone says something or does something to hurt us. Then we react. Everything in verse 31 is a reaction. Until we deal with these things, we will be in terrible spiritual condition. Are you there? You may be—if your trouble was brought on by people.

Verse 32 gives us three stepping stones on the pathway to freedom and victory. Paul begins this verse by saying, "And *be ye kind* one to another…" What a simple instruction. I do not know how often I have heard Ephesians 4:32 given as a memory verse for young children. Could I ask you to think about this question? According to this verse, to whom am I supposed to be kind? The typical answer is—everyone. That is true, but this verse is given in a particular discussion. Paul has just told us to get rid of bitterness, anger, wrath, etc. We have pointed out that these sins are reactions to people who have hurt us. It is in that context that Paul tells us to be kind to one another.

Who hurt you? The message of verse 32 is that you should be kind to that person. It may be that the person who hurt you is the last person to whom you feel like extending kindness. Now let's be careful here. There are some people we may need to avoid. Someone may have hurt you physically and may intend to do it again. Stay away from them, but pray for them. Also, realize that if there are legal or criminal issues, you have no obligation to help them avoid accountability for their sin or the appropriate consequences for their wrong. Aside from those kinds of situations, however, we should seek to be kind to those who have been unkind to us.

The world says, "I'll be kind to you, if you are kind to me." Christianity says, "I'll be kind to you, even if you are unkind to me." This challenge to be kind helps us get our lives on a spiritual level instead of an emotional level. Perhaps someone has betrayed you, spoken unkindly about you, sought to ruin your reputation with a lie, or has committed some other act that has brought you much pain within. Ask the Lord to give you an opportunity to be kind to them or to meet a need in their lives.

David's dealings with Saul form a convicting testimony of how we should deal with people who have turned against us. Saul sought to harm David and tried on some occasions to kill him. Time after time David responded in kindness. David had the opportunity to harm Saul and, in fact, could have killed him. He did not do it. In I Samuel 24:11–12 David spoke to Saul and said, "…know thou and see that there is neither evil nor transgression in mine hand, and I have not sinned against thee; yet thou huntest my soul to take it. The Lord judge between me and thee, and the Lord avenge me of thee: but mine hand shall not be upon thee." The Lord rewarded David. Eventually, Saul was off the throne, and David was on the throne; but it was the Lord's doing, not the vengeance of David. Let's go back to the first stepping stone and let the simple words sink deeply into our hearts—"And be ye kind one to another."

The second stepping stone in verse 32 is described with a single word, *tenderhearted*. There are too many hardhearted people in the world, and many of them are Christians. To be *hardhearted* means to be callous. I remember when I was a boy in school there was a kid in class whose hand was loaded with calluses. He loved to stick pins through the calluses and show everyone his hand. He wanted us to know he felt no pain. We get hurt, and we do not want to be hurt anymore. The inner pain has been too much for us, so we become emotionally callous and refuse to let anybody get close enough to hurt us. Just like those pins, the experiences of life are capable of creating pain, but the callus protects the tender areas. That is the way we are. We are not going to get close to people anymore and expose the tender areas that could feel pain.

I have heard people declare that they are not going to let themselves get hurt again. This is dangerous in many ways. If we are going to love someone, we will take the risk of getting hurt. If we are going to serve the Lord in any way, we will take the risk of getting hurt. No one wants to get hurt again, but you and I must be willing to be hurt again if we are going to be of any value to the Lord—and if we are going to have the human relationships that He intends for us. Have you developed a hardened heart? If so, it is extremely important for you to open up to the Lord and ask Him to give you a renewed tenderness. Tell Him you do not want anymore hurt; but tell Him you are willing to be hurt again, if it is His will.

There is often great excitement and expectation that accompanies love and life as we grow up. I can add to that the thrill of being called into the ministry. We look ahead with hope and anticipation of blessing and success. We imagine many wonderful experiences that we will enjoy. Eventually, however, hurts come to us all and the joy of serving Jesus can be tempered. At that point, we can pull away to protect ourselves from further difficulty or we can follow Scripture and press on in the sustaining grace of God. There are many who used to be happy, but they are not happy anymore. They used to be busy serving the Lord, but they do not serve much anymore. For some there is no church involvement at all because they experienced problems and do not feel it is worth the trouble to worship and serve with other believers.

Do you have a hardened heart? If you do, you know it. You may find security in having closed your heart to people and not letting anyone get too close, but that is a lonely pathway. Stop and ask the Lord to give you a tender heart so you can find renewed joy in loving people and serving Him.

The third stepping stone to freedom in verse 32 is *forgiveness.* Paul writes, "Forgiving one another, even as God for Christ's sake hath forgiven you." There are various views about forgiveness, but let's get a clear picture of what is taught in this verse. Forgiveness on our part is likened to God's forgiveness toward us. The key is "for Christ's sake." All forgiveness is based on the work of our Savior on Calvary—whether it be God's forgiveness toward us or our forgiveness toward someone else. The shed blood of the Lord Jesus paid the price for all our sin. Nothing else remedies the sin problem. Remember then that all of your sin (past, present, and future) was paid for at Calvary. Remember, too, that all the sin of the one who hurt you was paid for at Calvary. That truth is the emphasis of this text. It is for that reason that Paul selected the particular term he used for forgiving.

The word *forgiving* in Ephesians 4:32 means unconditional giving. The Bible is clear in this text and others that we are to forgive people when they sin against us. But what keeps us from forgiving? Usually it comes down to a few issues including: they do not deserve to be forgiven; they have not asked to be forgiven; or, possibly, they have asked for forgiveness, but we believe they are likely to commit the same kind of offense again. These excuses will not hold up. Waiting until someone deserves forgiveness may take years. Conditions for such forgiveness usually include demands that are beyond the ability of the offender.

How can he prove himself and make himself worthy? Would his efforts ever be enough? Does the Lord want us to wait years before forgiving? Think about it.

On the other hand, the offender may not desire forgiveness and therefore will never make an effort to earn our forgiveness. Do the Scriptures allow us to wait to forgive him? Surely if someone does seek forgiveness, the Bible teaches us in Matthew 18:21 and Luke 17:3–4 that we are obligated to forgive him and to accept his apology at face value, even if we think he will probably sin again. When all issues are considered we will find no excuse to refuse to forgive.

Let's take time to consider forgiveness more fully including the issue of confrontation. The Bible teaches the concept of going to confront one who trespasses against us. How does it work? Matthew 18:15–35 deals with the issue of sin against brethren and gives a pattern for us to follow. Briefly, it is this—Go tell the person his fault between you and him alone. If he does not respond properly, take someone with you. If he does not respond to the two of you, take it to the church. If he will not hear the church, he is to be treated as a heathen man and a publican. When in that passage (verse 21) Peter asked how often he had to forgive, the Lord Jesus said, "Seventy times seven." In Luke 17:3 the Lord Jesus told his disciples that if a brother sinned against them, they were to rebuke him. That means to challenge him or charge him. If he repented, they were to forgive him.

Questions that arise are "Do I have to confront a person who sins against me? Can I forgive someone who I do not confront and who does not seek forgiveness?"

It will help us to consider what forgiveness accomplishes and what it does not accomplish. Let's remember that whether we forgive someone or hold a grudge against them, it has no bearing on their fellowship with the Lord. Even if we forgive them, they still have to face Him. The issue of our forgiveness of others has to do with our ongoing relationship with them. Was the Lord telling us in Matthew and Luke that we could not forgive people of their trespasses against us unless we confront them? If so, we are going to be very busy people. People sin against one another often through word, deed, attitude, and action. Sometimes it is not a sin of commission, it is a sin of omission. In other words, it is not always what someone does, it is sometimes what they do not do. Must I confront them about every one of those instances which I believe to be sin? Can I not forgive them unless I confront them and they repent? In

I Peter  4:8 Peter wrote, "And above all things have fervent charity (love) among yourselves: for charity (love) shall cover the multitude of sins." I am glad for a love that covers sins. In other words, I am glad for a love that allows me to maintain fellowship with someone and forgive them, even when they sin. The reason we can do that is because judgment and vengeance are not our business—they are God's. I cannot relieve a man of his obligation to God, but I can relieve him of his obligation to me. And I can even do it without confronting him.

Consider the great challenge of Romans 12:19–21, "Dearly beloved, avenge not yourselves, but rather give place unto wrath: for it is written, Vengeance is mine; I will repay, saith the Lord. Therefore if thine enemy hunger, feed him; if he thirst, give him drink: for in so doing thou shalt heap coals of fire on his head. Be not overcome of evil, but overcome evil with good." Consider what this text means because it has bearing on the whole matter of forgiveness and helps us understand our third stepping stone on the pathway to freedom. The Lord tells us in verse 19 to not avenge ourselves because vengeance is His. He will repay. In simple terms, that means you can turn a person over to the Lord. He is the Lord's business. God will deal with him. He will repay. My challenge is to feed him and give him drink, if he has need. Does that sound like "Be ye kind one to another…"? It does to me.

What is the forgiveness of Ephesians 4:32 and how does it work? If someone sins against you, and you are being defeated through bitterness, anger, wrath, etc., you may need to confront him. If you can find no other victory, then you must go through the process of Matthew 18 and Luke 17. If, on the other hand, you can forgive him with *unconditional giving* as taught in Ephesians 4:32, you can be free of the list of reactionary sins of Ephesians 4:31—all of which grieve the Holy Spirit of God. If you refuse to forgive, who suffers? Only you. Some people will not forgive and will not confront. They may spend the rest of their lives being eaten up with bitterness, anger, and malice. Some people will not forgive until they confront. If it is necessary for you to confront your offender in order to find peace and get a matter resolved, do so—and do it carefully according to the pattern taught in Scripture. Others can find freedom in Ephesians 4:32. They can forgive without conditions, recognizing that their offender must still face the Lord and that the Lord will take vengeance, if vengeance is necessary. When forgiveness is extended to someone, freedom comes. There is no more bitterness, anger, evil speaking, etc.

What about you? Are you tired of the spiritual defeat and emotional burden that comes with living in verse 31? There may be someone in your present or past whom you need to forgive. If they are seeking forgiveness, your response will be a blessing to them. They still need to make things right before the Lord, but fellowship on a human level can be fully restored. When you forgive them, they will be free and so will you.

There may also be someone whom you need to forgive who is not seeking forgiveness. Your forgiveness toward them will do nothing for them, but it will still set you free. Do not wait for them to come to ask forgiveness because they may never come. Do not wait for them to achieve some level of Christian living where you think they will deserve forgiveness. Could that ever really be achieved? Do not wait until you think you can be sure they will never commit the same sin again. We never know what may show up in someone's life. If you must confront the person, do it quickly—but you can forgive them right now. Acknowledge to the Lord that you forgive the person and are relinquishing him into His hands because you realize vengeance belongs to the Lord, not to you. You can find peace when you entrust that person to the Lord, and when you do, the oppressive sins of Ephesians 4:31 will go from your life.

Take heart in these things. Forgiveness is not your way of saying what the person did is okay. It is not saying they are free to do it again. It is not saying the person is free from the consequences that might be appropriate such as church discipline, legal punishment, or the chastisement of the Lord. Forgiveness sets you free and puts them squarely before the God of heaven.

## CHAPTER ELEVEN

# RESTING IN HIS LOVE

One of the struggles that people face in time of trial is finding the peace to rest in God's love. Many have asked, "Why would a loving God…? If God loves me, why did he let this happen? Maybe I have done something that has caused God to not love me?" These questions and others that might be raised are answered in the text before us. In hard times we must rest in His love. We will not deal in detail with every verse of our text, but we must not fail to get its message. As Christians we are secure in the love of our Lord. Everything the Lord does directly and everything He allows to come into our lives will ultimately be used by Him for our good.

*Romans 8:18–39*

*18 For I reckon that the sufferings of this present time are not worthy to be compared with the glory which shall be revealed in us.*

*19 For the earnest expectation of the creature waiteth for the manifestation of the sons of God.*

*20 For the creature was made subject to vanity, not willingly, but by reason of him who hath subjected the same in hope.*

*21 Because the creature itself also shall be delivered from the bondage of corruption into the glorious liberty of the children of God.*

*22 For we know that the whole creation groaneth and travaileth in pain together until now.*

*23 And not only they, but ourselves also, which have the firstfruits of the Spirit, even we ourselves groan within ourselves, waiting for the adoption, to wit, the redemption of our body.*

*24 For we are saved by hope: but hope that is seen is not hope: for what a man seeth, why doth he yet hope for?*

*25 But if we hope for that we see not, then do we with patience wait for it.*

*26 Likewise the Spirit also helpeth our infirmities: for we know not what we should pray for as we ought: but the Spirit itself maketh intercession for us with groanings which cannot be uttered.*

*27 And he that searcheth the hearts knoweth what is the mind of the Spirit, because he maketh intercession for the saints according to the will of God.*

*28 And we know that all things work together for good to them that love God, to them who are the called according to his purpose.*

*29 For whom he did foreknow, he also did predestinate to be conformed to the image of his Son, that he might be the first born among many brethren.*

*30 Moreover whom he did predestinate, them he also called: and whom he called, them he also justified: and whom he justified, them he also glorified.*

*31 What shall we then say to these things? If God be for us, who can be against us?*

*32 He that spared not his own Son, but delivered him up for us all, how shall he not with him also freely give us all things?*

*33 Who shall lay any thing to the charge of God's elect? It is God that justifieth.*

*34 Who is he that condemneth? It is Christ that died, yea rather, that is risen again, who is even at the right hand of God, who also maketh intercession for us.*

*35 Who shall separate us from the love of Christ? shall tribulation, or distress, or persecution, or famine, or nakedness, or peril, or sword?*

*36 As it is written, For thy sake we are killed all the day long, we are accounted as sheep for the slaughter.*

*37 Nay, in all these things we are more than conquerors through him that loved us.*

*38 For I am persuaded, that neither death, nor life, nor angels, nor principalities, nor powers, nor things present, nor things to come,*

*39 Nor height, nor depth, nor any other creature, shall be able to separate us from the love of God, which is in Christ Jesus our Lord.*

In verse 18 Paul begins with a statement of great assurance. It is meaningful only if the reader is saved because it turns our hearts toward heaven. Many times in Scripture we are given comfort by being reminded that there really is a heaven, and, someday, we will be there. It will be wonderful, and in God's presence will be joy, peace, and blessing forevermore. As an added encouragement we are told that while present times may be tough, the sufferings now cannot compare to the glory to come. The blessings of heaven will more than make up for any suffering here on earth. That truth may be something you need to dwell on today. Thank Him for that truth. Ask Him to give you grace to handle your difficult circumstances.

In verses 19–22 Paul tells us that not only is full victory coming for us who are saved, but the whole sin-cursed creation will be delivered from its bondage of corruption. In verse 22 Paul says that the whole creation groans and travails in pain. What a picture of our world! The term *groan* means to agonize. The world system is in rebellion against God, but there is no peace. One person hates another; one nation attacks another. Greed, violence, immorality, and other sins hold the world in their grasp. People want happiness and never find it, unless they reject sin and come to the cross of Calvary to receive Christ as Savior.

Not only does the creation groan under the curse of sin, but the verse also says it travails. The term *travail* speaks of birth pains or as some call them—labor pains. When it is time for the birth of a child, the birth pains begin. At first they are gentle and far apart. As the time of birth gets nearer, they intensify in pain and come more and more frequently. Relief only comes when the child has been born. That is a picture of this world. The pain and agony is getting worse and worse. Wickedness and heartache are intensifying, but relief will only come when Christ delivers the creation from its bondage. Tragically, millions will die without Christ between now and then. They will spend eternity in hell.

In verse 23 he tells us that not only is creation in agony, but we are, too. Being saved, we have what Paul calls the firstfruits of the Holy Spirit. The Holy Spirit lives in us. His presence in us now is the firstfruits of our salvation. Having Him indwell us is like a taste of the full salvation to come. It is also a guarantee that we will get all the blessings the Lord Jesus provided for us when He shed His blood on the cross. However, the verse tells us we are waiting for the adoption, which he goes on to define as the redemption of our body. The full blessings of our salvation will not come until we get a new body. Give thanks to the Lord, we are not going to be in these present bodies forever. In these bodies there is pain, disease, injury, suffering, and finally death. We need to see this picture clearly. We live in a body that is in agony, subject to pain, sorrow, and death. We live in a world that functions under the intensifying curse of sin. Is it any wonder we have trouble in this life?

In verses 24–25 we are told that we are saved *by* hope. The idea is that our hope of full heavenly blessings is a part of what keeps us going in the hard times. If we could see all that awaits us, we would not need hope, but our hope of heaven gives us patience and endurance while we face the trials of this life.

In verses 26–27 Paul says that we not only have the indwelling presence of the Holy Spirit but we also have the assurance of His intercession when we pray. Paul says the Spirit helps our infirmities. Our infirmities are our human weaknesses. We are all very weak in ourselves. We cannot handle the pressures of life. We sometimes want to quit. In our frustration and fatigue we cry out to the Lord in prayer. But the truth is we really do not know what to ask. We do not know what needs to happen to solve a problem, change a situation, or change someone's life.

Here is a wonderful source of encouragement—when we pray, the Holy Spirit intercedes for us. He takes the burdens of our hearts and knows exactly how they should be put before the throne of our Heavenly Father. He pleads our case before the Lord. When He does, the Father, Who searches our hearts, receives the proper requests from the Spirit, which will be in harmony with the will of God.

Let's consider a simple illustration of how this wonderful ministry of the Holy Spirit might work in our lives. You have been praying for someone you know to change for the good. You do not have the slightest idea what it will take to make that happen. If he got sick, would he turn to God or get bitter? What if he lost his job? Would that turn him to the Lord? Maybe just the right person has to come along to talk to him in order for him to think more about spiritual things. Perhaps special blessings of good happening in his life may cause him to give God glory and draw him closer to the Lord. Maybe there is something totally different than you could even imagine that would humble him before the Lord. For what should you pray?

When you pray with your feeble and finite understanding of things, the Holy Spirit takes your burden and lays it before the Throne of Grace, in accordance with the will of God. You do not know what to pray. The Holy Spirit knows exactly what you should ask, and He intercedes for you. You need to be aware of how this works because thinking you know what needs to happen may drive you to ask for very specific things to occur that are not in harmony with God's will. When what you ask for does not happen, you may tend to believe that God did not hear or did not care. How wrong you would be.

Verse 28 now makes wonderful sense and brings incredible blessing. Because of our lack of understanding of the will of God and through the perfect intercession of the Holy Spirit, we can claim this promise. Paul says, "And we know that all things work together for good to them that love God, to them who are the called according to his purpose." We might think we know exactly what should happen to solve a situation. We don't! What may seem to be the wrong answer to our prayers may very well be the loving response of our Heavenly Father to the perfect intercession of the Holy Spirit on our behalf. He is working all things together for good for those who are saved.

Can you rest in that love? If you are going through a hard time, you may feel the Lord has not responded to your prayers. Just the opposite is true. The Holy Spirit has interceded on your behalf, and your Heavenly Father is at work. Can you rest in His love? There is no hope for victory unless you do.

In verses 29–34 Paul reminds us that we are secure in that love. He does so by presenting to us five great truths. The first is found in verses 29–30 where we are told that as Christians we are predestinated to be conformed to the image of Christ. In other words, come what may in this life, we will someday be like Him and nothing can hinder that from happening. That teaching is couched in a list of God's workings of salvation. Before you were saved, you were foreknown by God. Having foreknown we would be saved, He predestinated us to eventually be conformed to the image of Christ. Between that foreknowledge in eternity past and our conforming to the image of Christ in eternity future, a number of things happen.

To make it personal, here is what happened and will yet happen to you and me who are saved. Having predestinated us to be conformed to the image of Christ, He called us. That call was the work of the Holy Spirit drawing us to Christ. Having called us, He justified us. When in response to the convicting work of the Holy Spirit we placed our faith in the Lord Jesus, we were declared righteous by God; we were justified. Since we are justified, we will be glorified. Someday we will leave this world for heaven and receive a new glorified body. Nothing can get in the way of that pattern of events. Indeed, we are secure in the love of God.

The second truth teaching us about our security in God's love is found in verse 31. Paul very simply states, "If God be for us, who can be against us?" We are certainly not worthy of God's love and salvation, and there are enemies that would seek to destroy us—but there is an obvious answer to the question. Who can be against us? Some might be against us, but no one can ultimately succeed. The Devil is our accuser, but since God is for us, Satan's accusations cannot stand in the courts of heaven.

The third truth about our security in the love of Christ is an appeal to spiritual logic. It is found in verse 32. Paul asks that if God spared not His own Son for us (that is, in expressing His love He made the greatest sacrifice possible for our salvation) how could it be that He would withhold the lesser things necessary for our full salvation? "God so loved the world that He gave His only begotten Son" (John 3:16). Having given us His Son, we can be sure He will give us everything else we could ever need for a full and eternal salvation.

The fourth truth is found in verse 33 and again draws on spiritual logic. God has justified us. We are guilty of sin in ourselves and always will be. We are not worthy of salvation and, in ourselves, never can be. Yet, the Holy God of heaven has justified us because of the precious blood of our Savior. If the Holy God of Eternity has justified us, who else must be satisfied? No one!

Verse 34 gives us the fifth truth by challenging anyone who would condemn us. How could we now be condemned? It is none other than the Lord Jesus Christ who died for us. He paid the price for our sin. More than that, He is risen from the dead, which proved His death paid the sin debt. If it did not, Christ would still be dead because death is the wage of sin. Furthermore, the Savior is seated at the right hand of God, where daily the value of the cross of Calvary is applied to us. The Apostle John puts it this way in I John 2:1, "And if any man sin, we have an advocate with the Father, Jesus Christ the righteous." The writer of

Hebrews says, "Wherefore he is able to save them to the uttermost that come unto God by him, seeing he ever liveth to make intercession for them" (7:25). Praise the Lord, we can no longer be condemned by anyone. What greater evidence could there be that we are secure in the wonderful love of our Lord?

This brings us to a very important part of Paul's message. It is extremely vital for our spiritual and emotion well-being. Verses 35–39 deal with those faith-testing experiences of life that can bring us down to despair. Verse 35 asks a critical question. "Who shall separate us from the love of Christ…?" Have you ever felt separated from the love of Christ? Do you feel that way right now? Have troublesome times ever made you feel deserted by the Lord? Have you felt your prayers have gone unanswered? In your time of greatest weakness, have you felt like heaven was silent to your cries for help? Oh, the destructiveness of shaken feelings. Oh, the blessedness of steady faith!

*Nothing can separate us from the love of God.*

Paul lists for us some specific things that can make us feel we have been separated from the love of Christ. He asks, "…shall tribulation, or distress, or persecution, or famine, or nakedness, or peril, or sword?" These are the kinds of things that make us feel deserted when we go through them. In verse 36 he quotes from Psalm 44:22. It says, "For thy sake are we killed all the day long; we are accounted as sheep for the slaughter." The psalmist was writing to express his confusion and personal defeat in the face of terrible trouble. To his understanding there was no reason for the difficult times he was enduring. He could not figure out why God was allowing these things to come upon him and his people. In Verse 24 of the psalm, he asked God this question, "Wherefore hidest thou thy face, and forgettest our affliction and our oppression?" You may feel today as he felt then.

In Romans 8:37 Paul responds in faith and assurance. He says, "Nay…" The question again, "Who shall separate us from the love of Christ? shall tribulation, or distress, or persecution, or famine, or nakedness, or peril, or sword?" Paul's answer—Nay, or as we would put it, NO! Then he said, "…in all these things we are more than conquerors through him that loved us." There is no promise from the Lord that tribulation, distress, persecution, famine, nakedness, peril, or sword will never come to the child of God. It is important that we realize if any or all of those experiences do come, it is not an indication that God does not love us. It is in the midst of these very experiences that Paul says that "we are more than conquerors."

Our response to difficulties is often to ask why God would let this happen? Good question! We do not always know why. We do know we live in a wicked world. We do know we can be sure of heaven. We do know that the sufferings of this present time are not worthy to be compared with the glory that is coming. We do know that when we pray the Holy Spirit takes our prayers to the Throne of Grace with perfect intercession. We do know that we are totally secure in God's love. We do know that God takes all things and works them together for good to them that love Him. It is on these truths we must stand. These truths do not necessarily relieve the pain of the hour, but they strengthen our faith and enlarge our hearts for heaven. This world is not our home, and this world will never be a friend to the child of God. We are living in enemy territory, but we are secure in God's love.

In verses 38–39 Paul makes a final statement in this discussion. He says, "For I am persuaded, that neither death, nor life, nor angels, nor principalities, nor powers, nor things present, nor things to come, nor height, nor depth, nor any other creature, shall be able to separate us from the love of God, which is in Christ Jesus our Lord." The term *persuaded* suggests a considered and final conclusion. In other words, Paul says that he has given a great deal of thought to this matter and now has it firmly settled in his mind. Nothing can separate us from the love of God.

After giving us a list, Paul says, "Nor any other creature." That means nothing that is part of creation. There are only two categories of existence. The first is God, the Creator. The second is all that God has created. Paul says nothing God has created is able to separate us from the love of God, the Creator. Do not ever doubt God's love for you. We may not be able to understand all the Lord does, but we know He maintains an undying love for us. Yes, He loves you now, and He always will. Rest in His love!

# CHAPTER TWELVE

# CLAIMING THE VICTORY BY FAITH

Yes, you can have victory over your trial and suffering. It may not come in a moment, but you can have it—if you really want it. You are in a spiritual warfare and you will have to learn to battle in the spiritual realm. You will have to take God at His word, do what He says, and trust Him by faith for that victory. If you follow God's Word, you can enjoy victory that few Christians ever experience.

In this section we are drawing from the passages we have just examined to establish guidelines for response to trials. To some degree they have been put in a logical order of belief and action, but do not fret about a specific order of response. There is no formula for claiming your victory in Christ. Follow the Scriptures. There are things that we must believe, and there are things that we must do to gain the victory the Lord promises in His Word. You may not *feel* like doing these things, but if you really want victory, it awaits you along the pathway of faith and obedience.

Before going through these guidelines, let me remind you of a few truths you must accept. Earlier, we stated that the greatest test in a time of trial is not what we go through, but how we respond to it. If you are overcome by anger, worry, bitterness, frustration, or grief, recognize that the way out of your situation is through a proper spiritual response to your trouble. David wrote in Psalm 40:1–3, "I waited patiently for the Lord; and he inclined unto me, and heard my cry. He brought me up also out of an horrible pit, out of the miry clay, and set my feet upon a rock, and established my goings. And he hath put a new song in my mouth, even praise unto our God: many shall see it, and fear, and shall trust in the Lord." What the Lord did for David, He will do for you.

In our discussion of II Corinthians 4:7–18, I mentioned Dr. George Mundell and his impact on my life. One of the greatest things he ever taught was another truth to help get us through trials. I hope as you read it you will take time to meditate on it. Based on Hebrews 12:10–14 and other Scriptures, he said, "**I must see every person and every circumstance that ever comes into my life as the Holy Spirit of God coming to me through that person or through that circumstance to make me more like Christ.**" It is so easy to get focused on people and circumstances that we often miss the Lord. Seek the Lord. Look for His purpose and plan regarding what is happening in your life. If you seek Him, you will find Him. When you find Him, you will experience spiritual, emotional, and mental healing.

There is one more truth you must accept. If you are miserable for the rest of your life, it will be your fault. I know that may seem harsh, but I state it with great compassion and tenderness. I know how hurtful life can be. I know what people can do to each other. I know the heartache of losing loved ones and seeing dreams come crashing down. But we cannot live in defeat. With trust in the Lord and hope in our hearts, we must refuse to wallow in discouragement. In Psalm 42:5 the psalmist wrote, "Why art thou cast down, O my soul? and why art thou disquieted in me? hope thou in God: for I shall yet praise him for the help of his countenance."

With these thoughts before you, consider these guidelines for claiming victory in your time of trial. Do not think of them as a formula or a series of steps that must be taken in a certain order. In fact, not every one may apply to your current situation. They are a list of truths from the Word of God which we must believe and act on. Most of them will fit your situation and open the door to victory, which at the moment may seem impossible to achieve. We can expect the Lord to be faithful to His Word and faithful to us, who are His children. Let's see how to practically apply the Scriptures we have just examined.

### 1. Thank God for what has happened in your life. I Thessalonians 5:18

This may be the biggest step of faith you have ever taken in your Christian life, but the Scriptures are clear about this instruction. Philippians 4:6 says, "Be careful for nothing; but in every thing by prayer and supplication *with thanksgiving* let your requests be made known unto God." II Corinthians 4:15 says, "For all things are for your sakes, that the abundant grace might through *the thanksgiving of many* redound to the glory of God." I Thessalonians 5:18 says, "In every thing *give thanks:* for this is the will of God in Christ Jesus concerning you." In Ephesians 5:20 Paul challenges, "*Giving thanks always* for all things unto God and the Father in the name of our Lord Jesus Christ."

I know the struggle you may face as you consider this instruction, but observe it carefully. It is not a challenge to *feel* thankful for what has happened; it is a challenge to *give* thanks. It is not a challenge to thank God that things are not worse, i.e., "Thank you, Lord, for allowing me to break only one leg instead of both legs." It is a challenge to give thanks for what has happened in your life. We cannot see what God is doing and often cannot imagine why God would allow certain tragedies to occur, but by faith we must say, "Thank you, Lord, for that which has happened to me." I have seen the sick and dying, the abused and molested, the hurting and confused respond victoriously to this biblical instruction. It has opened the door to the outpouring of God's grace in their lives. I know how hesitant you may be but...do it! Thank you, Lord, for _____.

### 2. *Confess any known sin. I John 1:9; Psalm 139:23–24*

We are all sinners and we are told that as we sow, so shall we reap. It is possible that the trial you are facing is in no way related to specific sin you have committed. However, the psalmist says, "Search me, O God, and know my heart: try me, and know my thoughts: and see if there be any wicked way in me, and lead me in the way everlasting." We should pray the same prayer. Ask the Lord to show you, remind you, and convict you of any sin that may be in your life and which has never been properly confessed. As the Lord brings things to mind, confess them and determine, by God's grace, to forsake them. If you need to make things right with other people, determine to go and resolve matters with them. When you have done these things, accept God's forgiveness and ask Him to restore your joy. If you can honestly say there is no sin that could be the cause for your problems, accept your situation as a trial of your faith. Satan loves to find people with a weak conscience. He makes them feel guilty when there is no reason for guilt. Don't live there. Deal with sin as you find it in Scripture and as the Holy Spirit convicts you, but do not let the Devil play games with your mind and emotions.

### 3. Humble yourself before the Lord. Recognize there is a divine purpose. I Peter 5:5–6; Hebrews 12:10–11

"Lord, I submit myself to you." I have prayed that prayer many times, not knowing why certain things have happened and certainly not knowing how to get out of a difficult situation. There has been the blessing of wonderful peace through that simple act of yielding to the Lord. Put yourself in the Lord's hands. Cast yourself on His mercy. Tell Him you are willing for the fulfillment of His plan and purpose in your life generally and in the specific situation you are facing currently. Things do not just happen. The Lord always has purpose in everything He does and everything He allows. Submission to His will and way opens the door to His grace.

### 4. Reject self-pity. I Peter 5:9; Hebrews 12:12–13

Self-pity is a sure way to terrible defeat. "Why did this have to happen to me?...Why do these things always happen to me?...Nobody understands what I have been through....Other people never suffer the way I have suffered." The attitudes reflected in these questions and statements reveal pride and a self-centered life. If we take our eyes off ourselves long enough, we will find others who have suffered far worse. If we look at ourselves in light of God's standards of holiness, we will marvel that God ever allowed anything good to happen to us. For some reason we think we deserve an easy road. We foolishly compare ourselves with others and cannot believe that we do not have more possessions, more money, and less trouble than others who appear to us less worthy.

When Asaph finally dealt with his self-pity in Psalm 73, he made two significant statements. In verse 1 he said, "Truly God is good." When he was feeling sorry for himself, he did not believe that the Lord had been good to him. The second statement he made was recorded in verse 22. "So foolish was I, and ignorant: I was as a beast before thee." Yes, Asaph had been foolish and ignorant, but no more than you and I when we fall into the pit of self-pity. We must reject self-pity, because the Lord has been better, to all of us, than any of us deserve.

### 5. If people are involved, forgive them. They are not the real enemy. Ephesians 4:32 and 6:12

We must remember that ultimately people are not the enemy. They can harm our reputation by what they say, and they can harm us physically perhaps, but they cannot destroy the inner man. Satan is the enemy of the soul. We must remember that we wrestle not against flesh and blood. Forgiveness toward those who have offended us takes flesh and blood out of the conflict. Once we have forgiven people, we can stay focused on the spiritual battle. People cannot take our peace and joy, but the Devil delights to do it. Based on the teachings of Ephesians 4:30–32, Ephesians 6:12, and Romans 12:19, you must forgive the people who have hurt you. By an act of your will, forgive them now. It will set you free to claim victory in your own life. You cannot control what anyone else does, so do not let what others do control you. To fail to forgive will bring bitterness into your life, and you will be poisoned all your earthly days.

The Bible clearly instructs us to forgive others. In fact, the word translated *forgive* in Ephesians 4:32 means unconditional giving. Some people establish conditions that must be met before they will forgive, but we can forgive people without setting conditions. Forgiveness is based on the value of the shed blood of Christ. Your offender's sins were dealt with at the cross. That is the only place he can find the full forgiveness he needs, because all sin is against the Lord. Therefore, the one who offended you will not be exonerated by your actions. He must deal with God.

Forgiveness does not mean you condone what he has done, nor does it mean he will be pardoned from the consequences of his actions. We can forgive those who offend us. Our forgiveness toward them sets us free to learn what the Lord has for us to learn, instead of being consumed by the hurt. Vengeance is not ours; it is the Lord's. And He said that He will repay. There may be legal consequences that the offender must experience, which will not be relieved by our forgiveness. So, forgive the offender and put him in the Lord's hands.

If the offender comes back seeking forgiveness, we must forgive immediately—but do not wait for him to come back. He may never come back, and you will be defeated by his offenses for the rest of your life. If you cannot forgive your offender, you must confront him, as taught in Matthew 18. Take the high ground. Bow your head in prayer, choose to forgive the one who offended you, and declare it to the Lord. If you still have not done it, do it now!

## 6. Resist the Devil. I Peter 5:7–9; James 4:7

We are told in the Bible to resist the Devil, steadfast in the faith. That means to actively stand against him, using the Word of God as our weapon. If we take time to think about our trial, we will quickly recognize what Satan is trying to do to defeat us, and we will be able to identify how he would like us to respond. Even now, if I could talk to you, I would ask, "What do you think the Devil would like to accomplish in you through this situation? What do you think he would want you to do?" I am sure you could tell me. Instead of giving in to him, run to the Scripture to find God's promises of help and consolation and to find out what God wants you to do.

As we suggested before, find God's promises. Believe them, claim them, and do not let them go. They will make you "steadfast in the faith." To be *steadfast* means to be firm and solid, as a foundation upon which one might build. Satan wants to use trials to shake the very foundation of our lives. Our foundation is the Word of God. As you stand on God's promises, you will be able to resist and withstand the Devil's attacks. In the Word of God, you will also find guidance to know what God wants you to do. Actively stand against Satan. Do not let him win this battle. Take the time to find some specific verses that address your situation. If no verse seems to address your exact problem, find verses that give a principle on which you can stand. When the Lord Jesus was tempted, He drove Satan away by using Scripture. That is the same way we resist him.

## 7. Take control of your thought life. Philippians 4:8

This is certainly easier said than done, but it is a necessity for a couple of reasons. First, continually thinking about negative events or experiences of the past can only bring greater hurt to us. We make ourselves victims all over again every time we bring a hurtful situation back to our mind. As we think on such things, we intensify our emotions, whether they are hurt, fear, anger, or whatever. Determine to turn your thinking toward good things every time the problems of the past come back to haunt you.

Second, realize that fretting and worrying about the future may only bring discouragement and despair. If there are things you should do to affect the future, get to it. If things are out of your control, recognize that worrying will only defeat you and possibly ruin your physical health. The Lord Jesus told His disciples in Matthew 6:34, "Take therefore no thought for the morrow: for the morrow shall take thought for the things of itself. Sufficient unto the day is the evil thereof." Our Lord was not advocating irresponsibility. He was talking about worry over the things that are beyond our control. We are to do our best, and we are to do right; then we leave the rest in the Lord's hands.

Third, come back to the passage in Philippians which we have used to introduce this very important matter. The word translated *think* in verse 8 means to reckon, consider, or take into account. It implies that on the basis of our *thinking* we will form an opinion, develop an attitude, or contemplate certain action. How critical it is that we think according to the instructions of God's Word. If we do not think right (and many people do not), we will formulate wrong opinions, develop poor attitudes, and do many foolish things. We must take control of, and responsibility for, our thoughts. Start now. It will be a tough battle, but stay at it.

## 8. *Seek to learn the lesson God has for you. James 1:2–4; Hebrews 12:10–13; Romans 8:28*

Why did the Lord allow these trials in your life? No one can give you that answer except the Lord Himself. What can we know? Romans 8:28 says, "And *we know* that all things work together for good to them that love God, to them who are the called according to his purpose." Do you believe that? More importantly, do you believe that for you? The writer of Hebrews assures us that God allows hard times in our lives for our profit, to produce in us greater holiness and righteousness. Have your profited in any way from your heartache? James says our trials are intended to help us mature spiritually. Have you grown spiritually because of all you have endured? Do not let your suffering be in vain. Ask the Lord to help you grow spiritually through this difficult time and ask Him to teach you the special lessons that should come out of this experience. Out of something so negative, look and ask for the positives that the Lord alone can produce in your life.

## 9. *Commit yourself to do right, regardless of others. Hebrews 12:10–14; Philippians 4:9*

In facing your time of trial, you must make a commitment to do right, regardless of what others may do or say. Sometimes it is hard to know what is right, but when, through searching the Scriptures and getting godly counsel, you conclude what is right, you must do it. Our tendency is to react to what others do. In other words, we decide what we are going to do based on what the other person does, rather than based on biblical teaching.

Everything human about us wants to react against people who have hurt us. We want to vindicate ourselves, justify ourselves, and sometimes get back at the one who hurt us. I have been there and have had to run to the Scriptures for help. In I Peter 2:23 Peter tells us about our Lord Jesus, "Who, when he was reviled, reviled not again; when he suffered, he threatened not; but committed himself to him that judgeth righteously." Then later in the same book, Peter exhorts us to respond to others, "Not rendering evil for evil, or railing for railing: but contrariwise blessing; knowing that ye are thereunto called, that ye should inherit a blessing" (3:9). You and I must determine to do what is right and hang on to the hope of that blessing which we are going to inherit.

In responding to my trials involving people, I have tried to keep two things in mind. The first is that people cannot ultimately bring hurt to me by what they say or do, because I am in the Lord's hands. That is what Peter was telling us about the Lord Jesus. He "committed himself to him that judgeth righteously." The Lord will eventually make all things right; maybe here on earth, maybe at the Judgment Seat of Christ, but it will happen. Rest in that truth. The second thing I have tried to keep in mind is that the Lord's work and testimony are bigger than I am. I do not want to bring reproach on the Lord just to satisfy my own desire to vindicate myself.

Now, let me clarify this matter. Do what is right. Do what is biblical. You may be accused of being the cause of trouble because you did what you knew was biblically right. Do not let those accusations ever make you back down from doing the right thing. At the same time, do not do wrong to get back at someone who did wrong to you.

### 10. Ask for wisdom to know what to do, and then do it. James 1:5; Philippians 4:9

In the midst of his discussion on trial and trouble, James says, "If any of you lack wisdom, let him ask of God" (1:5). The challenge here is similar to the one we just gave in the last section, but I want to keep it separate to emphasize the pathway to wisdom. James tells us specifically to ask for wisdom. We need it desperately in a time of difficulty. The Greek term translated *wisdom* in this text is defined in *Vine's Expository Dictionary of Old and New Testament Words* as "insight into the true nature of things." It is the ability to see things as they really are. We cannot make good choices and decisions about matters if we do not see them clearly. That is one of the reasons the Bible tells us there is safety in a multitude of counselors.

When we face a problem, we may have a very narrow perspective or a bias that prejudices our view. Seeking counsel may help us see a matter with greater objectivity. Let me add that caution should be used in seeking human counsel since our advisors may have their own prejudices or fail to truly use the Bible as their guide. Better than human counsel is wisdom that we can get from God Himself. That is why James says if we lack wisdom, we are to ask of Him. Getting wisdom from God includes prayer and searching the Scriptures. Measure right and wrong by the Bible and nothing else. Evaluate a situation based on Scripture. When you see a matter in the clear light of the Word of God, you will have a basis for deciding what pathway you should follow in responding to your trial. As we stated in the last section, when you know what is right, do it and do it the right way.

### 11. Let your requests be made known unto God. Pray. Pray. Pray. Philippians 4:6; Luke 18:1–7

Unfortunately, prayer is one of those things we talk about, but seldom do to the degree that is necessary. In Paul's discussion about handling trial in Philippians 4, he talks about not worrying, thanking the Lord for what happened, thinking properly, and doing the right thing. Thankfully, he also includes our privilege to pray and ask the Lord to work in the troublesome situation. He says, "Let your requests be made known unto God." In this time of trial, what do you want, what do you need, what is your desire?

We should remember there is much teaching in the Bible to guide us in prayer. For instance, I am often reminded of Romans 8:26. It says, "Likewise the Spirit also helpeth our infirmities: for we know not what we should pray for as we ought: but the Spirit itself maketh intercession for us with groanings which cannot be uttered." That verse tells us that while we may know what we ultimately want to have happen, we do not know what needs to take place to bring it about. Let's suppose someone has been extremely unkind to you, and you want it to stop. You do not really know what to ask of God. Should you ask the Lord to have the person move away, change his heart, let you move away, or so strengthen you that his unkindness no longer defeats you? If you focus on a specific request, "Lord, make this person move away," that may not happen. The Spirit of God will intercede for you so that the things that need to happen, for you to have spiritual victory, will occur. Pour your heart out to the Lord. He cares and He will hear. Keep on praying.

The parable of Luke 18:1–7 will be very helpful. Turn to it in your Bible and read it. Take special notice of the purpose of the parable as given in verse 1. "That men ought always to pray, and not to faint (quit)." Take notice of the promise of comfort in verse 7. "And shall not God avenge his own elect which cry day and night unto him…?" *To avenge* means to vindicate, to make things right, to punish on behalf of the offended. So, pray, pray, pray, and tell the Lord the burden of your heart.

### 12. *Renew your eternal perspective. II Corinthians 4:14–18; Hebrews 12:1–3; I Peter 5:10*

Someday everything is going to be made right. This is a great truth which can serve to provide abiding peace when all seems to be going wrong. There is no doubt that Paul's eternal perspective sustained him during all his earthly trials. One of his more familiar statements is found in II Corinthians 4:17–18, "For our light affliction, which is but for a moment, worketh for us a far more exceeding and eternal weight of glory; while we look not at the things which are seen, but at the things which are not seen: for the things which are seen are temporal; but the things which are not seen are eternal." He makes a similar statement in Romans 8:18, "For I reckon that the sufferings of this present time are not worthy to be compared with the glory which shall be revealed in us." Yes, there is a day coming when the struggles will be over and the heartaches will be gone. As John puts it in Revelation 21:4, "And God shall wipe away all tears from their eyes; and there shall be no more death, neither sorrow, nor crying, neither shall there be any more pain: for the former things are passed away."

If you are saved, you will find great comfort and encouragement in the reality of your heavenly hope. The Lord Jesus has gone to prepare a place for us, and someday we will be home. Press on to serve the Lord. As the writer of Hebrews 12:1 puts it, "Let us run with patience (endurance) the race that is set before us." Right now, you might feel that you cannot go on. The Lord says you can. Thank the Lord for your salvation and ask Him to help you keep your eternal perspective in the midst of your current trial. It will be worth it all when we meet the Lord and see Him face to face.

### 13. Rejoice in the comforting presence of God. Philippians 4:4–7; Hebrews 13:5b

Along with our assurance of heaven in the future is our assurance of the comforting presence of God right now. In Philippians 4:5 Paul tells us, "The Lord is at hand." That is not only a reminder of the Lord's soon return, it is also assurance of His abiding presence with us now. The promise of Hebrews 13:5b is so wonderful. The writer quotes the promise of the Lord from the Old Testament saying, "I will never leave thee, nor forsake thee." As it was originally written, there is great intensity in the statement. We could read it this way, "I will never, never leave thee, and never, never, never forsake thee." Paul tells of his own situation as recorded in II Timothy 4:16–17. He says, "At my first answer no man stood with me, but all men forsook me...Notwithstanding the Lord stood with me, and strengthened me." Yes, it is as the psalmist wrote in Psalm 46:1, "God is our refuge and strength, a very present help in trouble.

Some people turn away from the Lord in their time of trouble. If you do not turn *to* Him, where do you turn? The Lord has not deserted you. He is right there with you. At one point in our Lord's earthly ministry, a very hurting man said in Mark 9:24, "Lord, I believe; help thou mine unbelief." The Lord did not rebuke that man; He answered his request. You might need to express those same words to the Lord. He will respond in tender compassion to you in your time of trial.

### 14. Enjoy the sweet victory.

If you trust and obey the Word of God, according to its teachings on how to respond to trial, you will open your life to sweet victory from the Lord. I want to remind you that victory does not always include a change in circumstances, but it will always include a change in you. When we take God at His Word and do what He tells us to do, we immediately avail ourselves of His abundant grace and peace. Comfort begins and our hearts are quieted before Him. We can have that peace that passes understanding.

We also avail ourselves of the Lord's day by day renewal of our inner man. One day at a time we will find the strength to go on. In Lamentations 3:22–23 Jeremiah wrote, "It is of the Lord's mercies that we are not consumed, because his compassions fail not. They are new every morning: great is thy faithfulness." Every new day will bring new mercy. Along with God's daily mercies to sustain us, we will also begin long term spiritual growth, gradually achieving new levels of spiritual, mental, and emotional stability. This is the healing process. As we are healed in these areas, we will actually be able to profit from our trials. That is God's promise.

We may gain some understanding of why the Lord allowed the trial in our lives, which, in turn, will hasten and enlarge our victory. We will develop a deeper commitment to doing right and reject the tendency to yield to sinful ways in our own lives. As we mature spiritually, we will deepen our faith so that we will be better equipped to handle troubles in the future. Things that used to defeat or anger us will not bother us nearly as much in the future.

As the Lord continues to work in us, He will restore peace, joy, and happiness in our hearts and renew our zeal to serve Him. He will take away the hardness of heart that is sometimes produced by trial, and He will replace it with the tenderness of heart that is necessary for full victory. There will also be the personal ministry of the Lord to you that will be unique to your need. The Lord understands how you feel and what you need. He will take very special care of you.

I realize the depth of your hurt may be keeping you from acting on the message of this book, but you must break through that hurt to respond spiritually to your trial. Please go back through this material as often as necessary to begin acting on God's Word and claiming the victory that only He can give you.

# CHAPTER THIRTEEN

# WHAT IF...?

Many who have been hurt are not getting victory. They are continuing through life in spiritual defeat. They are suffering, and so is everyone who is close to them. You must claim victory! Consider what awaits you if you do not.

Through Paul's victory recorded for us in II Corinthians 4:8–9, he escaped distress and despair. Distress is anguish and mental torment. Despair is hopelessness. You must escape these valleys of sorrow. Refuse to live there. Paul also conquered feelings of being forsaken. Hurt and failed by people, Paul found sustaining comfort in the awareness of God's presence and care. He also avoided being destroyed. The term *destroyed* is translated marred in Mark 2:22 where old wine skins were marred (destroyed) when they were filled with new wine and then burst. The wine skins still existed, but they were useless and never able to be used again for their intended purpose. Many people end up the same way. Their lives are meaningless and valueless to the Lord, themselves, and their loved ones. Do not let your life become a worthless existence. The Lord has far better things for you.

In Genesis 37 we read of the betrayal of Joseph by his brothers. Having cast him into a pit, they drew him out and sold him into slavery. His father was led to believe Joseph had been killed by a wild animal. Verse 35 says, "And all his sons and all his daughters rose up to comfort him; but he refused to be comforted; and he said, For I will go down into the grave unto my son mourning." Who could condemn him for his broken heart? About twenty years later a famine in Israel drew Jacob's family to Egypt to find food. Joseph, now governor of Egypt, recognized his brothers and demanded that Benjamin, his younger brother, be brought to Egypt. When Reuben told Jacob that Benjamin would have to go to Egypt, Jacob responded with these words, "My son shall not go down with you; for his brother is dead, and he is left alone: if mischief befall him by the way in the which ye go, then shall ye bring down my gray hairs with sorrow to the grave" (42:38). In the twenty years since the apparent death of Joseph, Jacob had found no peace nor comfort from the Lord. It was available to him, but he refused it.

In II Samuel 17:23 we read of a man named Ahithophel who tragically took his own life. He was the grandfather of Bathsheba. His anger and bitterness toward King David over David's sin against Uriah and Bathsheba moved him to offer counsel to Absolam that Ahithophel hoped would lead to David's death. The counsel was not followed, and Ahithophel's plan was foiled. Verse 23 says, "And when Ahithophel saw that his counsel was not followed, he saddled his ass, and arose, and gat him home to his house, to his city, and put his household in order, and hanged himself, and died, and was buried in the sepulchre of his father." We can understand his anger, but what was accomplished for God's glory or his family's well-being by his taking his own life? Did he not know that vengeance belongs to the Lord? Through Nathan the prophet, the Lord had already pronounced judgment on David's house. In II Samuel 12:10 Nathan spoke these sobering words to David, "Now therefore the sword shall never depart from thine house; because thou has despised me, and hast taken the wife of Uriah the Hittite to be thy wife." What might the balance of Ahithophel's life have been if he had drawn near to the Lord? How might he have been used? What blessings may have come out of his tragedy? We will never know.

In Hebrews 12:15–17 there are severe warnings for those who find no victory over trial and heartache. The threefold suffering includes bitterness, immorality, and profane living. Bitterness is described as a root. It is deep-seeded hostility, resentfulness, and animosity. A root is the source and feeder of plant life. The surface life is an evidence of the root and the result of being fed by the root system. If you have a root of bitterness, imagine the harsh words, outbursts of anger, or unkind and malicious deeds that may eventually be produced as its fruit.

Immorality (fornication) is also introduced as a result of defeat through trial. Discouragement can produce moral apathy. It takes spiritual alertness and concern to avoid falling into sin. Defeat brings vulnerability, and many have fallen victim to such devilish temptations.

A third result of defeat mentioned in Hebrews 12 is profane living. Profanity is the demonstration of irreverence and contempt for the things that are held in esteem by the Lord. Often feeling that the Lord is the source of trouble—He could have stopped it if He wanted to—the defeated person rejects the things of God and makes foolish and shortsighted choices. As with the example of Esau, given in the text, such choices may bring irreversible results. And, as with Esau, tears of sorrow may be genuine, but the consequences of the foolishness may be permanent. Esau sold his birthright to his brother, Jacob, because he had no regard for spiritual and eternal things. He had far more interest in what he wanted on the spur of the moment. Afterward—Do you remember as we stated earlier that there is always an afterward?— Afterward, when Esau would have received great blessing from the Lord, he was rejected for his foolishness and profane ways. I must tell you that God graciously allowed some blessing for Esau anyway, but it was far less than the Lord had originally made available to him. Will yielding to pressures or the desires of the moment cost you the greater blessing of the Lord?

No less than two other results of defeat through trial are mentioned in Scripture. The first is the wounded and hardened heart. God's peace can keep and guard the heart as mentioned in Philippians 4:7. The term *keep* is a military term which includes safety, generally, and protection from an enemy, specifically. The heart is the deepest part of our being, but it is vulnerable to attack. Terms like hardened heart, broken heart, blinded heart, troubled heart, and foolish heart are found in Scripture, in contrast to terms like pure heart, good heart, rejoicing heart, melodious heart, steadfast heart, and tender heart. How we need the God of peace to keep our hearts. Which of the above terms describe your heart right now?

Philippians 4:7 also tells us God's peace can keep or guard the mind. Never in history have more people had mind (mental) problems than today. Are all of these problems unavoidable? The term translated *mind,* in this text, is defined in *Vine's Expository Dictionary of Old and New Testament Words* as "speaking generally, the seat of reflective consciousness, comprising the faculties of perception and understanding, and those of feeling, judging and determining." How many people today are a mental mess, because of their trials? Their understanding has been blurred, they exercise poor judgment, and they make bad decisions. Why? Because they have missed out on the peace of God and have given in to inner turmoil. Have your problems driven you to mental confusion,

chaos, and disorder? You need peace, and it will only come from the
Lord through careful obedience to His Word.

I wish you would stop right now and take some time to honestly evaluate
your situation. What is the trial or trouble you are facing? What do you
think Satan has tried to do to you through this time? I emphasize *to
you,* to your inner man. What do you think the Lord may be trying to
accomplish in your life? Has Satan been successful? Has the Lord been
successful? How are you different now than you were before the trials
began? Surely, you are different. Is the difference spiritually positive
or negative?

Please, for your own sake and that of your loved ones, claim the victory.
The Scriptures are not filled with theory or good ideas. They are the very
Word of God. You can believe them, trust them, and follow them all the
way to the victory you desperately need.

# CHAPTER FOURTEEN

# THE BASIS OF HOPE FOR VICTORY

As you have read the pages of this book you may have noticed an underlying theme brought out in many passages of Scripture that talk about trials and our victory over them. In fact, to miss the truth of this theme will eliminate the possibility of true and lasting victory over trouble. The truths I am referring to are the wonderful realities of salvation through the Lord Jesus Christ. Unless you enjoy the blessed assurance of salvation and the eternal security that is ours in Christ, true victory cannot be claimed.

Let's consider the texts that relate eternal salvation with victory over trial. Then we will discuss the whole matter more fully.

One of the first texts we looked at was II Corinthians 4:7–18. It is in verse 14 that Paul begins his discussion on how to get victory. He says, "Knowing that he which raised up the Lord Jesus shall raise up us also." Paul had been describing many difficult situations that he had faced. He made it known that some of the circumstances were not going to change. Often our hope for victory is tied to our hope for situational change. There is nothing wrong with asking the Lord to change situations, and many times He does. Paul's victory, however, was founded upon the truth that he was some day going to be raised from the dead, and then he would have ultimate and permanent victory. Changes in the here and now could not be guaranteed. Eventual change in heaven was guaranteed. In that truth Paul found peace and joy. Do you have the same assurance that Paul had? Do you know without any doubt that someday you too will be raised from the dead to enjoy the presence and blessings of God forever?

In Philippians 4:5 Paul wrote, "Let your moderation be known unto all men. The Lord is at hand." In our discussion of this verse we emphasized the phrase "The Lord is at hand" as referring to the presence of the Lord. He is with us always. We also mentioned, however, that this brief sentence holds the promise of the return of the Lord Jesus. He is coming again. Here is a question. Is there any value in believing that the Lord is coming back if His return will not usher in our eternal blessing? If He is coming back—and you are one of those who are left behind—there is no comfort in the promise of His return. Are you sure that if He returns today to take His own to heaven that you will go, too?

Consider the glorious truth of Romans 8. We cannot rehearse it all again, but think with me on the familiar text of verse 28. "And we know that all things work together for good to them that love God, to them who are the called according to His purpose." The victory statement is that all things work together for your good. When you believe that, you can find great peace in the midst of circumstances that bring you hurt. The foundation of that hope for victory is the assurance that all things work together for good to certain people. It is not for everybody, but it is for them who are called according to His purpose. It is in knowing we are called according to His purpose that we can grasp the reality that life and the meaning of life's experiences will find ultimate fulfillment in eternity. You may not see everything worked out now and may not understand all of life while you are still on the earth, but you will finally see it when the eternal purpose of God is fulfilled in heaven. Your present trials are included in His eternal purpose for you. Only this precious truth could stir Paul to write in verse 18 of the same chapter, "For I reckon that the sufferings of this present time are not worthy to be compared with the glory which shall be revealed in us."

In Hebrews 12 we put our emphasis on how to handle trials and the need to avoid self-pity as seen in verses 10–15, but the writer gave us an added message in verses 6–8. He told us that the Lord chastens those He loves, and if we endure chastening, the Lord is dealing with us as sons. The term *son* speaks of kinship and is contrasted with the term *bastard* which speaks of being illegitimate. In fact, he tells us that if we do not experience chastisement, we are not sons. As the text tells us later, God knows that life can bring much hurt, but we go through the troublesome times as the child of a loving heavenly Father. He will use those experiences to teach us and train us toward Christlikeness. Knowing we are children of God gives us strength and encouragement. He is with us and will never forsake us.

Peter included the same truths about salvation in his writing on the topic of gaining victory over trial. In I Peter 5:10, as he discussed our response to trial, he wrote, "But the God of all grace, who hath called us unto his eternal glory by Christ Jesus..." The same God who offers us the sufficiency of His grace is the one who has called us to eternal glory. The hope of eternal glory became the basis of hope throughout the time of trial. If God's grace is enough to bring about an eternal salvation, it will certainly be enough to sustain us through the times of temporal trouble.

Paul challenged us in Ephesians 4:32 to be kind and tenderhearted. Then he told us to forgive one another even as God for Christ's sake had forgiven us. How could we ever forgive as God has forgiven us, if we have never experienced the delivering power of God's forgiveness in our own lives? No person can truly and fully forgive another, unless he has been forgiven. Oh, the sweetness of God's forgiveness! Oh, the joy to be set free on the basis of the shed blood of the Lord Jesus! To fail to understand that our own forgiveness is founded on that shed blood will keep us from grasping that His shed blood paid the price for all sin, for all men, for all time, and especially for the sin of those who may have sinned against us. That is why we can forgive others. They may not deserve it, but the price has been paid. If you are saved, you know you do not deserve God's forgiveness; and while you had to seek it, you would have never come to Him unless you were drawn through the gracious work of His Holy Spirit in your heart. Only those who have been forgiven by the Lord can truly forgive others. Do you have full certainty that you have received God's forgiveness for your sin?

One final text I saved until last is Hebrews 12:2, "Looking unto Jesus the author and finisher of our faith; who for the joy that was set before him endured the cross, despising the shame, and is set down at the right hand of the throne of God." We are told to look unto Jesus to see how to find victory. He endured the cross. None of us have gone through anything that could compare to His sufferings and, as we know, He was totally innocent of any sin or crime. He despised the shame. The term *despise* means to think down or think against something. It suggests we consider something as slight or valueless. The cross was everything, but the shame that came with it meant nothing to Christ. The cross was too important to have its value mitigated by the shame of His public suffering at the hands of men. Why could the Savior of the world endure the cross whereon He bore our sins? For the joy that was set before Him. Heaven was a reality for the Lord Jesus. He had come from heaven and would shortly return to heaven. What joy would be His! Now the text reminds us that He is there at the right hand of the throne of God. His heavenly joy is restored. Some day you too will be in heaven if you are saved through faith in Jesus Christ. What joy it will be! If you can grasp some of that reality now, you will endure your cross for the joy that is awaiting you.

Why is it necessary to be saved and sure of it in order to gain full, complete, and lasting victory over earthly trials? The Scriptures are clear in their teaching. The experience of men through the ages demonstrates that not all problems will be solved on this side of eternity. Not all sickness will be healed. Death will come to all, except those who live until the actual day of the Lord's return. Many evil people will never pay a fitting price for their sin and wickedness while they live on the earth. When will justice be meted out? The teaching of the Bible is very plain on this matter. There is a time coming for every person to stand personally before the Lord Jesus Christ. At that time each individual will receive personal judgment that will be in perfect harmony with what he deserves, based on the righteousness of the holy God of heaven. Those who are not saved will be cast into the Lake of Fire which was prepared for the Devil and his angels. Not only will each go to the Lake of Fire, but in that place of suffering each will receive the judgment that is perfectly matched to his sin and rebellion against God, as well as his sin against other people.

Addressing that judgment the Apostle John wrote in Revelation 20:13, "And they were judged every man according to their works." We can rest in that truth. There is a day coming when everything will be made right. Every injustice committed on this earth will be addressed. All that has been wrong will be rectified. That is why Paul wrote in Romans 12:19, "Dearly beloved, avenge not yourselves, but rather give place unto wrath: for it is written, Vengeance is mine; I will repay, saith the Lord." The Lord knows far better than we do, what should happen to make things right. We might wish something terrible on one person and think another deserves mercy. God may see it quite differently. The Lord knows all things and will judge perfectly. That is the way it is going to be. However, if you are not saved, there is no consolation to be found in future judgment. Unsaved people experience hard times here on earth and then still face God's judgment at the Great White Throne of Revelation 20. As they see others receive judgment and justice, they too will receive the wrath of God.

For someone who is saved, the story is totally different. When the Lord
Jesus Christ died on the cross of Calvary something happened that is
beyond human comprehension. Listen to the Bible's description from
both the Old and New Testaments. Isaiah described it in the 53rd chapter
of his book. He wrote in verses 4–6, "Surely he (Christ) hath borne our
griefs, and carried our sorrows: yet we did esteem him stricken, smitten
of God, and afflicted. But he was wounded for our transgressions, he
was bruised for our iniquities: the chastisement of our peace was upon
him; and with his stripes we are healed...the Lord hath laid on him
the iniquity of us all." In the New Testament we read Paul's words in
II Corinthians 5:21, "For he (God) hath made him (Christ) to be sin for
us, who (Christ) knew no sin; that we might be made the righteousness
of God in him." Peter put it this way in I Peter 2:24, "Who (Jesus Christ)
his own self bare our sins in his own body on the tree (cross)...by whose
stripes ye were healed." When Jesus Christ died, it was not the hand of
man that brought His greatest suffering—it was the hand of God. God
the Father put our sin and its appropriate punishment on the Lord
Jesus. He suffered and died as a substitute for us.

These words remind us that all of us are sinners before God and that
all of us deserve God's wrath. We may think our wrong doing is far less
than someone else's and that we deserve a better life than what we have
experienced, but not one of us is innocent. When we face the reality
that we are not only victims of the sin of others, but are also guilty of sin
before God, we can appreciate the love of the Lord Jesus for us. He loved
us so much that He became sin for us and suffered the punishment on
the cross of Calvary that we would otherwise receive at the Great White
Throne judgment. Justice was meted out for our sin, but the Lord Jesus
took the punishment. For the saved to meet Him face to face will not
bring His eternal wrath. As His children we will be judged to evaluate
how we have served Him since being saved—but our place in heaven
will be secure. The judgment of the Christian will bring reward for
faithfulness to the Lord rather than punishment for sin.

Being saved makes the believer God's child—makes him the special
object of God's love and care—includes the promise of God's presence
and the promise that God will never allow more trial than He will enable
us to bear. It secures a heavenly home where sin will be no more, tears
will be wiped away, and pain, sorrow, and death will be eliminated
forever. It is the absolute certainty of these eternal blessings that the
writers of Scripture use to encourage us toward victory. As Paul puts it in

II Corinthians 4:17, "For our light affliction, which is but for a moment, worketh for us a far more exceeding and eternal weight of glory."

If you are not saved or are not sure you are saved consider this brief explanation.

Some people commit more and greater sins than others, but before God we are all equally deserving of eternal punishment. Since the punishment will be perfectly matched to the sinner and his deeds, some will suffer in eternity more than others. The first issue to be faced, however, is that we are all worthy of punishment because we all far short of the glory of God. God is holy and demands holiness from those who would abide in His eternal presence. Whether you sin one time or a thousand times, sin in any degree misses the standard of holiness. If we compare ourselves with other people, we may find some whom we think are better than ourselves and others whom we think are worse. If we compare ourselves to the Lord, we are guilty.

Because God is holy, He must judge sin and therefore condemn the sinner. But God is also love as stated in I John 4:8. In His love He devised a plan to express His love for all, while judging sin for all. John 3:16 explains it this way, "For God so loved the world, that he gave his only begotten Son that whosoever believeth in him should not perish, but have everlasting life." There it is. The Son of God, our Lord Jesus Christ came to this world to die so those who would believe in Him should not perish, but have everlasting life."

With the coming of and death of Jesus Christ the issue of salvation was moved from man's sinfulness to man's response to Jesus Christ. The Lord Jesus paid the price for sin. Now the question becomes whether people will believe on Him. To reject Him leaves people with no payment for their sin, so they have to face the wrath of God at the Great White Throne judgment. To receive Him makes one a true child of God with sin paid for by the Lord Jesus. John 1:11–13 says, "He came unto his own, and his own received him not. But as many as received him, to them gave he power to become the sons (children) of God, even to them that believe on his name: Which were born, not of blood, nor of the will of the flesh, nor of the will of man, but of God."

Many have misunderstood the message of salvation. Some have taught that to be saved is related to church attendance or being a member of a particular church. This is false teaching. Others have related salvation to various kinds of religious practices and participation in certain ordinances or sacraments. Still others try to convince people that it will take a high level of good living and kindness toward others to win salvation. Still more would teach that any religious beliefs and practices are sufficient to get one into heaven as long as they are carried out with sincerity. These teachings turn our eyes away from the reality of the matter. No good works or religious activities can pay the price for our sin. God's Word teaches clearly that we are so far from being able to merit salvation that He offers it as a free gift to any and all who will receive it. Paul wrote in Ephesians 2:8–9, "For by grace are ye saved through faith; and that not of yourselves: it is the GIFT of God: Not of works, lest any man should boast." The message Paul gave to the believers at Ephesus was the same one that he gave to those at Rome. In Romans 6:23 he wrote, "For the wages of sin is death; but the GIFT of God is eternal life through Jesus Christ our Lord."

These truths are not difficult to understand. All of us are sinners before a holy God. Sin must be paid for. Since God loved this world, He sent His Son to die on the cross of Calvary. There Jesus Christ paid for our sin and received the punishment from God that we deserved. From that time until the end of time the question for mankind is—What will each person do with Jesus Christ? Will people receive Him or reject Him? Will we accept the offers of His mercy and grace, or will we try to reach God in our own way and on our own terms?

What does someone do to get saved? How does someone receive Jesus Christ and the gift of eternal life? When you accept the truth that you are a sinner before God and, therefore, worthy of due punishment for sin, you acknowledge that you are spiritually lost. That is important because the Lord Jesus says in Luke 19:10, "The Son of man (Jesus Christ) is come to seek and to save that which was lost." Jesus Christ came seeking to save you. In I Timothy 2:3–4 Paul wrote, "For this is good and acceptable in the sight of God our Savior; Who will have all men to be saved, and to come unto the knowledge of the truth." Peter wrote in II Peter 3:9, "The Lord is...not willing that any should perish, but that all should come to repentance." Let it be settled that the Lord is willing for you to be saved. You need to come to repentance, which means you need to turn from your sin. Sin is wrong; it is destructive; it is transgression of God's law; it is an offense to God. In turning from sin you must turn to the Lord Jesus Christ and believe on Him as your Savior. The Apostle Paul commended new believers in I Thessalonians 1:9–10 when he reminded them that many knew "how ye (they) turned to God from idols to serve the living and true God; And to wait for his Son from heaven, whom he raised from the dead, even Jesus, which delivered us from the wrath to come,"

To accept the free gift of salvation we can follow the instructions of the Apostle Paul given in Romans 10:9-13, "That if thou shalt confess with thy mouth the Lord Jesus, and shalt believe in thine heart that God hath raised him from the dead, thou shalt be saved. For with the heart man believeth unto righteousness; and with the mouth confession is made unto salvation. For the scripture saith, Whosoever believeth on him shall not be ashamed. For there is no difference between the Jew and the Greek: for the same Lord over all is rich unto all that call upon him. For whosoever shall call upon the name of the Lord shall be saved."

Belief in the heart is what you believe in the deepest part of your being. Confession of the mouth is your expression of your belief to God. If you believe on Christ, you will not be ashamed; and if you believe, you can be sure the Lord will hear you, accept you, and give to you the spiritual riches of His salvation. Call on Him. If you were lost physically and you knew someone came to seek you, you would call out to him. As one who is spiritually lost you can call on the One who came to seek and save you. Confess to Him your sinfulness, confess to Him your belief that He paid the price for your sins, and acknowledge that there could be no other way for you to be saved but through Him and what He did on Calvary's cross. Confess to Him your belief in His resurrection from the dead. Call on Him to save you as an expression of the belief you have in your heart, because as the text says, "Whosoever shall call upon the name of the Lord shall be saved."

Once a person is saved, life and even the troubles of life take on new meaning. Being saved brings new purpose for living and a new perspective on every experience endured. A saved person is no longer a victim of Satan, sin, circumstances, or people; but now a servant of the living God— now ready to believe the promises of God's faithfulness—now ready to claim the victories that are found in Christ. David wrote in Psalm 40:2, "He brought me up also out of an horrible pit, out of the miry clay, and set my feet upon a rock, and established my goings." That is Christianity at its best, and it is available to you. Claim it and live it by the grace of God.

# APPENDIX

# DEPRESSION

*Getting Help from Scripture*

# DEPRESSION

*Getting Help from Scripture*

More people are diagnosed with depression today than ever before. It is estimated that at any one time as many as 6% of the population of the United States is in a state of depression. Depression has been called the *common cold* of mental illness. The World Health Organization has predicted that depression will be the leading cause of disability and premature death in the industrial world by the year 2020. It is a topic that must be addressed by Christians, and it needs commentary and evaluation based on the Scriptures. Let it be emphasized that this writer is not a psychologist, psychiatrist, nor a worker of any kind in the common setting of mental health professionals, but is a student of and preacher of the Word of God. The Bible does not address every aspect of depression as it is described and defined by today's medical community. It does, however, show us various people who experienced depression. It shows us how they got into their depressed state and, in some instances, shows us how they got out of it.

Let's give a few preliminary comments before looking directly at Scripture. There is sufficient evidence to show that sometimes depression may be related to a physical cause. Someone battling depression may have a vitamin deficiency, nutrient deficiency, thyroid problem, low blood sugar, chronic pain, hormonal problems, or a chronic illness. Anyone who struggles with depression for more than a few days at a time would be well advised to seek advice and counsel from their family doctor. Tests may reveal a condition that can be relieved through good medical care. Addressing the physical problem may relieve the tendency toward depression.

Studies have shown, however, that the strongest predictors of liability to major depression, especially among women, are stressful life events. Included in the list are loss of a parent, lack of social support, loss of a job, and break up of a relationship. Experiencing these kinds of emotional strains can be very hard on anyone. These are the kinds of experiences that are recorded in Scripture.

Before we go any further there should be a **warning** given here. It may be that as you read this section of the book you may become convinced that if you have been on some medication you do not need it any more. **DO NOT**, I emphasize, **DO NOT** stop taking medications that a doctor has prescribed for you, unless the doctor agrees. **DO NOT** reduce dosages without your doctor's agreement. If you are married, it would be appropriate for you to also discuss such matters with your mate. I have heard of some people who have become convinced their problems were purely spiritual and, therefore, thought their problems should be handled spiritually. Some of these folks have stopped or reduced medication on their own and have ended up with greater difficulties.

**DO NOT** adopt the view that if you are on medication for depression you are less of a person or a poor testimony for the Lord. The medication you are taking will not hinder you from addressing any spiritual or emotional aspects of your circumstances. If you believe your medications are too heavy for you to function properly, consult your doctor and let him decide about any changes that may be appropriate. If you get complete victory, your doctor will recognize it and be glad to reduce or eliminate medication. With these words of caution in mind, let's take a further look at depression.

What is depression? Depression may be described in various ways. Usually the following terms are used to help us understand it. A depressed person will be in a state of melancholy. There will be sadness and low spirits. There will be a doom and gloom attitude and feelings of dejection. There may be an inability to concentrate and loss of motivation. Sometimes there may be insomnia and even thoughts of suicide. Depression is psychological pain. It is no happy experience to be depressed.

Can the Scriptures help us? Absolutely! The Bible introduces us to a number of people who suffered from depression. We can see what contributed to their problem and see how many of them got victory over it.

*Consider Elijah in I Kings 19:1–19. Please open your Bible and read the text.*

In verse 4 Elijah's depression is clearly revealed. Elijah sat down under a juniper tree and asked the Lord to take his life. What brought him to this point of despair? Just a few days earlier (I Kings 18:19–40) Elijah had been in a great conflict with King Ahab and the prophets of the false god, Baal. Elijah won the battle as the fire of the Lord fell from heaven and consumed Elijah's sacrifice, as well as the altar on which it was laid. Elijah gave instruction for the prophets of Baal to be killed. Elijah then climbed to the top of Mount Carmel and prayed for rain, which had not fallen in three and one half years. He came down from the mountain and, in the midst of a terrible storm, ran about 26 miles to the city of Jezreel. There he waited for the arrival of Ahab. Without question, Elijah was totally exhausted, physically and emotionally.

In verse 1 we are told of Ahab's arrival at the palace of Jezreel. He went in and told his wicked queen, Jezebel, all that had occurred at Carmel. Elijah waited outside for her response. It appears Elijah had fallen into a common emotional trap. In his mind he had built great expectations of what was going to happen when Jezebel heard the report from Ahab. He thought she would give up and surrender. He was sure the Lord was going to secure a dramatic victory for righteousness and turn the whole nation around. Instead the report brought out by Jezebel's servant was a threat to take Elijah's life within 24 hours. Elijah was stunned and seemingly unable to maintain his trust in the power of the Lord. He ran for his life and went ninety miles south to Beersheba. There he left his servant and went another day's journey into the wilderness of Sinai. When we find him in verse 4, he is quoted as saying, "It is enough." In other words, he said, "I cannot take it anymore." Have you ever been there?

In this record of Elijah's defeat are common elements that lead to depression: physical weariness, emotional exhaustion, and unfulfilled expectations. The proverbial straw that broke the camel's back was Elijah's belief that the Lord was going to bring Ahab and Jezebel to their knees. The problem was that the Lord never told Elijah that was going to happen. Elijah built up a picture in his own mind of what he thought God was going to do. When the Lord did not fulfill Elijah's expectations, Elijah gave up. That was all he could take. As Christians we are to give our all for the cause of Christ, whether in our personal life, married life, or family. Our tendency is to build expectations of what we think should happen as a result of our efforts. When we feel like we have given everything, but things do not go our way, we can feel we have been treated unfairly. We set ourselves up for a terrible fall.

It is extremely important to take note of the Lord's response to Elijah. You can read it in verses 5–7. The Lord sent an angel to minister to Elijah. He prepared him food and drink and encouraged him to sleep and get the rest he needed. He did not rebuke him nor belittle him for his wavering faith. The Lord understood all the factors that led to Elijah's personal struggle. The Lord will not be sending an angel to prepare food and drink for you and me, but we can be sure of the Lord's same compassionate awareness of our weakness. His ministry to us will be to comfort, not condemn. Elijah said he wanted to die. He did not really want to die. He was discouraged and saw no way out of his circumstances. That is where many people end up today. When we see no light at the end of the tunnel, when there is no apparent help or hope, anyone can be brought to the point of despair. It is then that we must run in faith to the Lord. His arms are open to us. He will not turn us away.

We must continue on, however, to get the full picture. Once Elijah had recovered from his exhaustion and was rested sufficiently to renew his service for the Lord, the Lord challenged him to serve again. Unfortunately, Elijah's unfulfilled expectations left him angry and filled with pride and self-pity. He rejected the Lord's tender appeal and walked away from complete surrender to the Lord. You can read this part of Elijah's experience in verses 8-18. Though he had a continued role in the Lord's work, it was not what it could have been if he had gotten full victory. You and I can be sure that the Lord will minister to us when we are hurting. His ultimate goal is to prepare us to serve again. Receive the comfort He offers. Run to Him—do not turn away from Him.

### Consider Ahithophel in II Samuel 17:23.

The text says, "And when Ahithophel saw that his counsel was not followed, he saddled his ass, and arose, and gat him home to his house, to his city, and put his household in order, and hanged himself, and died, and was buried in the sepulcher of his father."

What a terrible tragedy occurred in this man's life. He did not have to end his own life, but he chose to do so. Why? Ahithophel was a well-respected counselor of King David and later of Absalom when Absalom rebelled against David. Ahithophel laid out a plan for Absalom that was designed to bring about the death of David. Another counselor named

Hushai convinced Absalom that Ahithophel's plan was not good, so Absalom rejected Ahithophel's ideas. Ahithophel was so defeated that he went home and took his own life.

What is behind this terrible scenario? In II Samuel 11 we read of David's sin with Bathsheba. In verse 3 we are told that Bathsheba was the daughter of Eliam. In II Samuel 23:34 we find Eliam listed as one of David's mighty men. We also find he is the son of Ahithophel. In other words, Ahithophel was Bathsheba's grandfather. Imagine the heartbreak of this man when he found out that the king he had served and respected had taken his granddaughter to commit his wicked adulterous sin.

Ahithophel had carried his anger and bitterness for over twelve years when he saw his chance to take vengeance on David. David's own son had rebelled against him, and Ahithophel thought he could lead an army of men against David to kill him. When his plan was rejected, his bitterness could not be relieved. It had eaten away at him for a long time and now it would destroy him.

The greatest tragedy in this story regarding Ahithophel is that he never took his burden to the Lord. He was determined to take personal vengeance on David. He did not grasp that vengeance belongs to the Lord. The Lord was making David pay an awful price for his sin, but Ahithophel did not trust the Lord and took things into his own hands. Did Ahithophel hurt David by what he did to himself? Of course not. He only brought greater heartache to his son, Eliam, and his granddaughter, Bathsheba. Ahithophel's story is a solemn reminder that we must stay very close to the Lord to resist the pressures that can take us down into a depressed state.

### Consider David is Psalm 32:3–4.

The text says, "When I kept silence, my bones waxed old through my roaring all the day long. For day and night thy hand was heavy upon me: my moisture is turned into the drought of summer. Selah."

David wrote Psalm 32 in response to his guilt and eventual forgiveness over his sin with Bathsheba. Verses 3–4 tell of the guilt he experienced before he confessed his sin. They present a picture of depression. He tried to hide his sin in a number of ways, but his conscience pounded within his soul. The guilt was too great, and it finally broke him. God's hand was heavy upon him leading him into spiritual drought. How do you commune with the Lord and find comfort in Him when your heartache has been caused by disobedience to Him? David's bones waxing old may speak of physical pain and discomfort that accompanied his inner conviction.

In Psalm 51 (which is also a psalm dealing with David's confession of his sin with Bathsheba) he says in verse 8, "Make me hear joy and gladness; that the bones which thou hast broken may rejoice." In verse 12 we read the familiar words, "Restore unto me the joy of thy salvation; and uphold me with thy free spirit."

Unconfessed sin and its accompanying guilt can bring on depression. Caught in our sin, but unwilling to confess it and make things right with others, can bring unbearable sadness and melancholy. Fear of the consequences of our sin can bring the destructive feelings of doom. David found freedom when he opened his heart to God and surrendered again to His will.

### Consider another text from God's Word, Proverbs 12:25.

The text says, "Heaviness in the heart of man maketh it stoop: but a good word maketh it glad." *Heaviness* speaks of sorrow, care, anxiety, and fear. In the heart of man, it makes the heart stoop. *Stoop* conveys depression. The term can speak of bowing down in worship, but here it is bowing down in defeat and brokenness. Here we are taught that fear, sorrow, and anxiety can produce depression. The text tells us the heart can be made glad by a good word. The good word may very well be the Word of God, but it is clearly the message of help and hope to relieve the heaviness, whether human or divine.

The clear message of the Bible is that depression is real, and it may have many sources. It could result from anger, bitterness, unfulfilled expectations, guilt, fear, or sorrow. We also saw that emotional and physical exhaustion can greatly contribute to our defeat. So what do we do? When depression comes and lasts for any period of time, there may need to be a medical evaluation to see if there is a physical cause. If a doctor discovers a vitamin deficiency, low blood sugar, or any of the typical physical causes, a wise person will submit to the recommended treatment.

In conjunction with that medical evaluation, certain questions should be asked. When did the depression begin? What were the surrounding events that may have contributed to the emotional and possible spiritual defeat? I have asked many people the simple question—What is wrong? On numerous occasions the response has been, "I don't know." When situations have so lent themselves, I have responded with conviction that the person does know what is wrong. Proverbs 14:10 says, "The heart knoweth his own bitterness." The question is, will the person open up and talk about it?

Depression, as seen in Scripture, came from experiences that could have been clearly identified and addressed. Elijah knew what was wrong, but he continued in anger with the Lord because he wanted things his way, not God's way. Ahithophel knew what was wrong. He had developed a hatred for David and he could not get back at him. David knew what was wrong. He was guilty over terrible sin and did not want to admit it and face the public shame that would come with its unveiling.

I am convinced that most people know what is wrong. Of our three biblical examples only David faced his problem and got complete victory, including deliverance from his depression. Ahithophel went into total defeat and took his own life—he did not have to do that. Elijah seemed to follow the pattern of most believers. He survived and gave God modest service, primarily carrying out judgment on Ahab and his family; however, Elijah never went on to serve the Lord as he could have and should have.

Facing the reality of our circumstances is critical to our success in getting complete victory over our problem. Depression is not a disease, it is a symptom. To get victory we must identify the cause. If the deeper problem is something physical, it must be addressed. If the problem is emotional or spiritual, then that issue must also be addressed. These words are not intended to oversimplify the matter. This is serious business. The failure to handle things properly brought Ahithophel to the point of taking his own life. Let's recognize there is a battle raging over our emotional, mental, and spiritual well-being. The Scriptures clearly address these issues as we have shown in the main body of this book. When one gets saved, there is the need for total transformation. Salvation makes one a born again child of God, but that is the beginning of spiritual life and is necessarily followed by growth and spiritual development. Understanding life and how it works needs to be adjusted. The thought life must be brought into obedience. Emotions must be controlled. Decision making must be guided by scriptural precept and principle. Even the body must be brought into subjection. These things can only be accomplished as we take in God's Word and submit to its teachings. We must live surrendered to the indwelling Holy Spirit, Who applies Scripture to our hearts and enables us to live for Christ.

It will be more difficult for some than for others. We all have a sinful nature, but some will have a greater disposition toward some sinful weaknesses, while others will have greater leanings toward others. The answers, however, are the same. We must grow. From whatever our starting point may be, we must move toward emotional stability through life victory, wise decision making, and Christlikeness in attitude and action. Herein is our defense against depression and our pathway out of it.

Do not settle for being a victim of these joy-killing, life-destroying plagues upon the inner man. Victory will not come in a moment. Weaknesses may linger for a long time, but determine to enter into the battle to reclaim your mind and your emotions. When you are confident any physical problems have been eliminated or addressed, claim God's victory and begin to battle back to claim the joy, peace, and happiness that are rightfully yours in Christ.

# BIBLIOGRAPHY

Strong, James. *Strong's Exhaustive Concordance of the Bible.* Hendrickson
     Publishers.

Vine, W.E. *Vine's Expository Dictionary of Old and New Testament Words.*
     Fleming H. Revell Company: Old Tappan, NJ. 1981.